SKILLS DEVELOPMENT IN UZBEKISTAN
A SECTOR ASSESSMENT

DECEMBER 2022

ASIAN DEVELOPMENT BANK

 Creative Commons Attribution 3.0 IGO license (CC BY 3.0 IGO)

© 2022 Asian Development Bank
6 ADB Avenue, Mandaluyong City, 1550 Metro Manila, Philippines
Tel +63 2 8632 4444; Fax +63 2 8636 2444
www.adb.org

Some rights reserved. Published in 2022.

ISBN 978-92-9269-891-1 (print); 978-92-9269-892-8 (electronic); 978-92-9269-893-5 (ebook)
Publication Stock No. TCS230023
DOI: http://dx.doi.org/10.22617/TCS230023

The views expressed in this publication are those of the authors and do not necessarily reflect the views and policies of the Asian Development Bank (ADB) or its Board of Governors or the governments they represent.

ADB does not guarantee the accuracy of the data included in this publication and accepts no responsibility for any consequence of their use. The mention of specific companies or products of manufacturers does not imply that they are endorsed or recommended by ADB in preference to others of a similar nature that are not mentioned.

By making any designation of or reference to a particular territory or geographic area, or by using the term "country" in this document, ADB does not intend to make any judgments as to the legal or other status of any territory or area.

This work is available under the Creative Commons Attribution 3.0 IGO license (CC BY 3.0 IGO) https://creativecommons.org/licenses/by/3.0/igo/. By using the content of this publication, you agree to be bound by the terms of this license. For attribution, translations, adaptations, and permissions, please read the provisions and terms of use at https://www.adb.org/terms-use#openaccess.

This CC license does not apply to non-ADB copyright materials in this publication. If the material is attributed to another source, please contact the copyright owner or publisher of that source for permission to reproduce it. ADB cannot be held liable for any claims that arise as a result of your use of the material.

Please contact pubsmarketing@adb.org if you have questions or comments with respect to content, or if you wish to obtain copyright permission for your intended use that does not fall within these terms, or for permission to use the ADB logo.

Corrigenda to ADB publications may be found at http://www.adb.org/publications/corrigenda.

Cover design by Rocilyn L. Laccay.

Notes:
In this publication, "$" refers to United States dollars.

Note on names of ministries of the Government of Uzbekistan: This publication refers to ministry names current when the content was completed. Changes were later announced in the Decree of the President of the Republic of Uzbekistan No. 269, *On measures to implement the administrative reforms of New Uzbekistan* (21 December 2022), to take effect in January 2023. The new ministries under this restructuring related to the discussion in this publication include the Ministry of Employment and Poverty Reduction and the Ministry of Higher Education, Science and Innovation. Other government agencies referred to in the publication may also have been affected.

Contents

Tables, Figures, and Box	v
Foreword	vii
Message from the Ministry of Employment and Labour Relations of the Republic of Uzbekistan	viii
Message from the Ministry of Higher and Secondary Specialized Education of the Republic of Uzbekistan	ix
Acknowledgments	x
Abbreviations	xi
Executive Summary	xii

I.	**Introduction**		1
	A.	Purpose and Scope	1
	B.	Methodology and Structure	1
	C.	Economic Context and Recent Developments	2
II.	**The Uzbekistan Education Sector**		13
	A.	Structure of the Education Sector	13
	B.	Education Enrollments: Overview	16
	C.	Secondary General Education (Grades 10–11)	16
	D.	Transition to Technical and Vocational Education and Training	18
	E.	Technical and Vocational Education and Training Enrollments	21
	F.	Curriculum	26
	G.	Teaching Staff	27
	H.	Facilities and Equipment	29
	I.	Assessment	31
	J.	Graduates	31
	K.	Quality Assurance	32
	L.	Private Technical and Vocational Education and Training	32
	M.	Financial Resources	32

III.	**Challenges and Opportunities**	37
	A. Demand for Technical and Vocational Education and Training Programs	37
	B. Linking Demand for Technical and Vocational Education and Training with Demand for Skills	38
	C. Learning Outputs: Quality	38
	D. Continuing Vocational Education and Training	45
IV.	**Labor Market Outcomes**	47
	A. Labor Market: An Aggregate Picture	47
	B. The Demand Side	48
	C. The Supply Side	49
	D. Matching Supply and Demand	49
V.	**Strengthening the Relevance and Quality of Technical and Vocational Education and Training in Uzbekistan**	51
	A. Demand for Technical and Vocational Education and Training and TVET Enrollments	51
	B. Careers Education and Guidance	52
	C. Curriculum	53
	D. Teaching Staff	55
	E. Facilities and Equipment	57
	F. Implementation	58
	G. Assessment	59
	H. Graduates	60
	I. Quality Assurance	61
	J. Continuing Vocational Education and Training	63
	K. Governance and Management	65
VI.	**Development Partner Assistance to Technical and Vocational Education and Training and the Labor Market**	68
VII.	**Conclusion**	71
	Glossary	73

Tables, Figures, and Box

Tables

1	Macroeconomic and Social Indicators	2
2	Enrollment Rates by Age and Gender in Formal Education, Academic Year 2017/2018	16
3	Enrollments in Grades 10 and 11, Academic Year 2018/2019	16
4	Number of Students by Type of Education	17
5	Population Change, by Age Group, 2000–2017	19
6	Admissions to and Graduation from General Education, Academic Years from 2011/2012 to 2015/2016	19
7a	Enrollments, Admissions, and Graduations, Technical and Vocational Education and Training Colleges, Academic Years from 2012/2013 to 2016/2017	19
7b	Enrollments, Admissions, and Graduations, Technical and Vocational Education and Training and Academic Lyceum, Academic Years from 2017/2018 to 2020/2021	20
8	Progression from Grade 9 to Technical and Vocational Education and Training and Academic Lyceums with Higher Education Admissions, from 2011/2012 to 2015/2016	20
9	Possible Progression Scenario from Grades 9 to 10, Technical and Vocational Educational Institutions, and Academic Lyceums	22
10	Distribution of Students at Technical and Vocational Education and Training Colleges, by Subject Sphere, Academic Year 2016/2017	23
11	Enrollments in Technical and Vocational Education and Training Colleges by Field of Study, Academic Years from 2011/2012 to 2016/2017	24
12	Professional Levels of Technical and Vocational Education and Training Teachers, 2017 and 2019	28
13	Technical and Vocational Education and Training Teachers and Masters in Five Priority Sectors, as of 1 August 2019	28
14	Age Distribution of Technical and Vocational Education and Training Teachers and Masters, 2017	29
15	Geographic Distribution of Technical and Vocational Education and Training Colleges and Enrollments, Academic Year 2016/2017	30
16	Technical and Vocational Education and Training Graduate Placements in Academic Year 2016/2017	31
17	Education Recurrent Budget Expenditure, by Sector, 2005–2016	34
18	Education Recurrent Budget Expenditure, by Sector	34
19	Total Budgetary and Nonbudgetary Expenditure on Education	36
20	Employers' Suggestions for Improvements to the Technical and Vocational Education and Training Curriculum	40
21	Employers' Suggestions for How to Improve the Quality of Teaching	42
22	Employers' Suggestions for How to Improve Cooperation	42
23	Employment and Internship Data for Technical and Vocational Education and Training College Graduates, 2011–2016	49
24	Moving from Policy to Practice	67
25	Development Partner Assistance to the Technical and Vocational Education and Training Sector	69

Figures

1	Organizational Structure of the Uzbekistan Education System	14
2	Uzbekistan Education Structure from Academic Year 2019/2020	15
3	Age Composition of Resident Population of Uzbekistan	18
4	Trends in Postsecondary Student Enrollments	21
5	Comparison of Current Expenditure on Education	33
6	Government Expenditure on Three Education Subsectors as a Percentage of Gross Domestic Product	35
7	Government Expenditure on Education Subsectors as a Percentage of Government Expenditure	35
8	Simple Calculation of per Capita Expenditure by Sector, 2012–2016	36
9	Skills Required by Employers	40
10	Employer Responses on Their Use of Different Recruitment Processes	44
11	Types of Training Delivery Considered in the Employer Survey	46
12	Competency-Based Curriculum Approach	53
13	The Knowledge, Skills, Attitude Model of Competence	53
14	Quality Improvement Cycle for Technical and Vocational Education and Training	62

Box

Development Strategy of the New Uzbekistan for 2022–2026	6

Foreword

Skills development as a pathway to employment and entrepreneurship is a crucial element in the building of societies. The potential for an individual's growth and ability to contribute to their community and society as a whole is directly related to the scope and depth of the skills they possess. We are living in an age of rapid technological innovations, evolving climate change, and influential health hazards. Each of us needs to have the technical and soft skills to manage our daily lives and our work, as well as to meet the challenges of shifting work requirements and opportunities. This is as true for Uzbekistan as for elsewhere, and the needs are great for Uzbekistan as it is diversifying its economy under internationalization, shifting to prolonged value chains for its resources, and preparing for the opportunities and challenges brought by the fourth industrial revolution (Industry 4.0). A key to successful skills development is ever-increasing collaboration between the public and private sectors, between employers and education and training service providers, and between policy makers and skills development practitioners.

The Asian Development Bank has supported this assessment as part of its overall support to the strengthening and development of the Uzbekistan technical and vocational education and training (TVET) sector. This report provides background data and analysis on the system and considers the impact of recent reforms, as well as global events, on the delivery of TVET. It discusses options for developing initial technical and soft skills in the formal education system for general education graduates, as well as delivering upskilling and reskilling services for the existing workforce and unemployed people. It highlights areas for improvement of the inherited TVET system in the country and provides examples of internationally recognized processes and mechanisms that could be adapted to meet Uzbekistan's specific requirements. It calls for improvements in quality and relevance of skills development through enhanced private sector participation in shaping competency-based learning and assessment. Furthermore, it links labor market and employment issues to the skills delivery systems and considers labor migrants' needs for relevant and recognized qualifications.

I hope this report is useful for an Uzbek audience, including all stakeholders in the policy making, planning, and delivery of skills development, and also that lessons learned could inform those who work on skills development across the region.

Yevgeniy Zhukov
Director General
Central and West Asia Department
Asian Development Bank

Message

A major challenge for Uzbekistan is to ensure employment for some half a million young people entering the labor market each year. At the same time, we are diversifying the economy through the development of the private sector, especially small and medium-sized enterprises, who are the main job creators. Retraining of unemployed people and upskilling of the workforce is one of the key strategies to strengthen labor productivity; boost economic competitiveness; improve employability for the young generation, women, and disadvantaged people; and better prepare people who are seeking jobs abroad.

This report examines the provision of formal training, retraining, and upskilling services in Uzbekistan, and provides insights into options for transforming and strengthening the skills development systems and processes to respond to labor market needs. It analyzes skills development from the point-of-view of the labor market, the collaboration between the public and private sectors, especially in specifying and providing skills required in line with the industrial processes. This report introduces a range of strategies and mechanisms that have been adopted successfully elsewhere and invites the reader to reflect on the best options for tomorrow's Uzbekistan.

Our aim is to encourage employers, industry associations, trade unions, and technical and vocational education and training practitioners and policy makers to understand their roles as stakeholders in the planning and delivery process of skills development, and to provide them with ideas on how to fulfill their roles, for example, through the establishment and enhancement of sector skills councils, and through active involvement and participation in training, internship, and assessment processes.

Erkin Mukhitdinov
First Deputy Minister
Ministry of Employment and Labour Relations of the Republic of Uzbekistan
August 2022

Message

To meet our national goal of achieving the status of an upper-middle-income country by 2030, we must diversify and modernize our economy, focusing on new technologies and building value chains based on the principle of "raw materials to finished products." At the same time, we are aiming for digital transformation in the public sector by developing e-transactional services and greater online citizen engagement. Both require strengthening the quality and delivery of vocational and professional education in the new technologies.

This report provides an overview of the Uzbek initial and continuing technical and vocational education and training (TVET) system, as well as recent developments of the system. It covers the relevant areas such as the status of the vocational education and training institutions, the necessary areas for improvements under the requirements of competency-based training, and the way for linking to the labor market. It also provides some analysis of the effects of the coronavirus disease (COVID-19) pandemic and taps on how the TVET system can contribute to our nation's preparation of the young generation to catch up with the trend of Industry 4.0.

We hope that policy makers and TVET practitioners will leverage on the report's different options for system development and improvement at the TVET institutional level, as well as regional and national levels. The report also aims to stimulate more interactive collaboration between industry, TVET practitioners, and government in the planning for needed skills, as well as mechanisms to ensure the high quality and relevance of training and promote improved competency-based assessment and recognition of both formal training and lifelong learning.

Komiljon Karimov
First Deputy Minister
Ministry of Higher and Secondary Specialized Education of the Republic of Uzbekistan
August 2022

Acknowledgments

This assessment of the skills development sector in Uzbekistan was prepared by a team of international and national consultants and Asian Development Bank (ADB) staff as part of technical assistance project (TA 9256-UZB) Skills Strategies for Industrial Modernization and Inclusive Growth. The consulting team consisted of Nigel Billany, Thomas Kinch, Alexander Siboni, Jean Duronsoy, and Omon Narzikulov, while the ADB team consisted of Norman LaRocque, Xin Long, Farida Djumabaeva, Jenevieve Rivera Javier, Jocelyn Narciso, Rose Ann Dumayas, Gladys Ann Maravilla, and Laureen Felisienne Tapnio.

This report summarizes the current situation in the skills development sector in Uzbekistan. It also outlines key government strategies that have been introduced to improve the ability of the sector to meet emerging challenges and highlights possible directions for reform. The report provides an analysis of the reforms introduced since 2016 related to the skills development sector and, more broadly, to public education. The report has been updated with reference to the impact of the coronavirus disease (COVID-19) pandemic on economic and education policies, with special reference to the associated acceleration toward the fourth industrial revolution (Industry 4.0).

The report team is grateful to the Ministry of Employment and Labour Relations, the Ministry of Higher and Secondary Specialized Education, regional administrations and other government agencies, all of whom have contributed openly and actively to discussions and who have shared data and perspectives on the sector. We also appreciate the efforts of the authors of many previous studies and analyses of the education system in Uzbekistan—their indirect inputs to our analysis have been invaluable.

The authors are grateful to Rie Hiraoka, director, Social Sector Division of the Central and West Asia Department, ADB; and Cindy Malvicini, former country director, ADB Uzbekistan Resident Mission, for their guidance and encouragement. ADB's Uzbekistan Resident Mission provided extensive logistical and administrative support.

Abbreviations

4IR	fourth industrial revolution
ADB	Asian Development Bank
ALMP	active labor market policy
AY	academic year
CBT	competency-based training
CEG	careers education and guidance
COVID-19	coronavirus disease
CPD	continuing professional development
CSSVE	Center for Secondary Specialized Vocational Education
CVET	continuing vocational education and training
FEZ	free economic zone
GDP	gross domestic product
HEI	higher education institution
ICT	information and communication technology
IT	information technology
iVET	initial vocational education and training
KOICA	Korea International Cooperation Agency
MOELR	Ministry of Employment and Labour Relations
MOF	Ministry of Finance
MHSSE	Ministry of Higher and Secondary Specialized Education
MSEs	micro and small enterprises
NOS	national occupational standard
NQF	national qualifications framework
OCS	occupational competency standard
PES	public employment service
PPP	public–private partnership
PTC	professional training center
QA	quality assurance
SDG	sustainable development goal
SQF	sector qualifications framework
SSC	sector skills council
TA	technical assistance
TVEI	technical and vocational educational institution
TVET	technical and vocational education and training
UPK	school production and training units
WBL	work-based learning

Executive Summary

Uzbekistan is continuing its reforms for structural transformation and diversification of the economy by shifting from a commodity-dependent to a competitive and industrialized economy. With an increase of more than 30% in the working age population projected by 2030, anticipating and addressing labor market challenges is a government priority. Uzbekistan is one of the youngest countries in Asia, with almost 60% of the population under the age of 30. It requires a high rate of job creation and well-functioning labor markets to absorb this economically active population. Transformation of the economic sectors has created new demands and new opportunities for technical and vocational education and training (TVET) at both the initial and the continuing levels. This report focuses on assessment of the status and the future needs for TVET and documents the possible ways forward for the government and the private sector to work together to create a modern TVET system in Uzbekistan, including strategies to alleviate the impacts of the coronavirus disease (COVID-19) pandemic on the economy and on skills development.

The assessment is based on analysis of secondary data, reports, and documents from central government ministries and agencies, complemented by workshops, focus group discussions, and an employer survey. Field trips to three regions allowed local-level interactions with employers, TVET teachers and management, and local government officials. Recent reforms in both the education sector and the labor market are also analyzed.

Uzbekistan's skills development system is challenged on several fronts, including quality and relevance: only 21% of respondents in the employer survey said that the education and training provided by TVET colleges was *relevant*, 32% said it was *not relevant*, and the remainder responded that it was *partly relevant*. Employers also reported that inadequate workforce skills pose a significant obstacle to business growth. Other evidence shows a mismatch between the number of graduates in different fields of study and the number of jobs created for both specialized secondary school and higher education graduates.

TVET was established as a separate education subsector in Uzbekistan in 2000. TVET is largely financed and delivered by the public sector, with support from various development partners. International support tends to be focused on specific trades, with limited contribution to overarching and systemic solutions, though the sector lessons learned have proved to be very useful for policy development. There is a small private sector, mostly focused on qualifications in the areas of languages, information and communication technology (ICT), and accounting. All TVET institutions (professional schools, professional colleges, and *technikums*), although administered by different line ministries, are overseen by the Ministry of Higher and Secondary Specialized Education (MHSSE), delivering qualifications to the Uzbekistan national qualifications framework (NQF) levels 3 and 4 (in professional schools and professional colleges), or to NQF levels 4 and 5 (in *technikums*). Some of the professional colleges and *technikums* are administered by different line ministries or companies.

The initial vocational education and training (iVET) comprises (i) professional schools and *technikums* administered by MHSSE, and (ii) professional colleges and *technikums* administered by line ministries or companies. Continuing vocational education and training (CVET) is under the Ministry of Employment and

Labour Relations (MOELR), which is responsible for delivering training programs through Welcome to Job (Isghga Markhamat) centers (or "monocenters"), professional training centers (PTCs), and vocational training points. Entry to professional schools (2-year programs) is an option on completion of grade 9 and leads after 2 years to either labor market entry or further study at a professional college (up to 2 years) or *technikum* (at least 2 years). Grade 11 graduates may apply directly to the professional college or the *technikum*. *Technikum* graduates may also apply directly to the university. In 2021, enrollment of grade 9 completers was about 79,000 students into 339 professional colleges or *technikums*, and about 160,000 students into 555 professional schools and 73 academic lyceums, while about 360,000 opted to continue in general secondary education to grade 11.

In Uzbekistan, the number of economically active women remains considerably lower than the number of economically active men (45.7% for women against 54.3% for men). The labor market displays clear gender patterns, with women predominating in lower-paid social sector jobs, and men predominating in technical and other higher paid fields. Women have fewer options to work at formal jobs or to start their own businesses and women in rural areas are much less competitive in the labor market. Similarly, unemployment rates in Uzbekistan show distinct gender patterns, and the official unemployment rate for women is consistently higher than for men.

Uzbekistan's medium-term strategic planning was encompassed in the National Action Strategy on Five Development Priority Areas 2017–2021, and the Development Strategy of the New Uzbekistan for 2022–2026 was approved in January 2022. Changes in Uzbekistan's economic priorities related to COVID-19 recovery plans mainly focus on strengthening industrial competitiveness and increasing energy efficiency. The future of work in the post-pandemic world will have a focus on equality of opportunities, digitalization, continuous lifelong learning, reskilling, and upskilling to keep skills relevant in a changing world. Consequently, the needs for ICT sector development and the accelerated application of cyber-physical production systems' approaches to manufacture (moves toward Industry 4.0) serve as a reason for reassessing ICT training programs and their delivery.

The private sector in Uzbekistan plays a key role in the economy, contributing almost 57% of gross domestic product (GDP) in 2016. The participation of the private sector in skills development policy dialogue is being expanded from direct involvement in only a few subsectors to industry-wide involvement with the recent establishment of sector skills bodies, for example, to contribute to the development of the occupational competency standard (OCS). In Uzbekistan, micro and small enterprises (MSEs, firms with up to 200 employees) are estimated to represent more than 99% of all enterprises and employ more than 77% of all workers. The needs of MSEs differ sharply from those of large enterprises, including greater challenges in identifying skills needs and fewer resources and opportunities for in-house training of their employees. However, TVET program quotas are linked to regional development planning, in which large employers are involved. Furthermore, the Government of Uzbekistan has identified entrepreneurship as a key focus for industrial modernization and job creation. But careers education and guidance (CEG) is weak and does not ensure that students choose training and education that is in accordance with what they are able and willing to engage in and what is in line with possible labor market opportunities.

Curriculum content and delivery are examined in-depth, with proposals on how to make them more relevant, as well as on the ways to reskill and upskill TVET teaching staff. TVET institutions are often equipped with basic (Industry 2.0) facilities and equipment, but major investments are needed to train students for 21st century needs, for example, in the construction, ICT, and automotive fields. New assessment systems are being developed against the OCS, especially for those participating in CVET programs, including certification of existing competencies, and it is anticipated that these new procedures will also be standardized for use in the elective professional training institutions.

The Uzbekistan NQF was approved in 2020. It is linked to an educational qualifications' framework and an OCS framework. Sector qualifications frameworks (SQFs) are being drafted for various sectors, but a clear need remains for additional inputs to the fledgling systems, as well as support for nationwide application, especially in terms of the skills requirements of Industry 4.0, where progression to cyber-physical production systems and technologically advanced environments requires systematic training of ICT users for increased digital literacy in all areas of the economy.

Funding for iVET is partly fee-based: TVET is provided free of charge to students in professional schools, but other TVET institutes charge fees, where students will pay for tuition and some other costs, although there are exceptions for those from poor households and for mitigating the impact of COVID-19. Opportunity costs of TVET previously were not an issue as TVET was part of the 12-year compulsory education (i.e., 9-year basic education plus 3-year TVET or 3-year study in academic lyceums) prior to the reform starting in 2017. However, with the onset of elective TVET, opportunity costs now become a factor. Funding for CVET under MOELR is under the government budget, with a view on the monocenters and PTCs eventually becoming self-financing.

Challenges, Opportunities, and Recommendations

Quality improvement for TVET. Support is needed to provide TVET programs with better balance between theory and practical work, more relevant nontechnical as well as technical skills, entrepreneurship as a cross-cutting domain, and better-monitored work practice and internships, thus changing the entire TVET system into a learner-oriented and competency-based delivery system. Further work is needed on skills needs analysis, preparation of the OCS, and establishment of a skills monitoring system to provide students with skill sets relevant to the evolving needs of the economy. All learners should, thus, learn from a modern, competency-based curriculum delivered through better-qualified teaching staff and with strengthened links between the educational system and private sector employers. Broader and deeper dialogue is needed between the economic sectors and the TVET system, at both central and institutional levels.

School-to-work transition. New graduates, in addition to acquiring needed knowledge and skills to increase their employability, shall learn how to write curriculum vitae (CVs), interview techniques, job information seeking; where to get adequate labor market information; how to register in the public employment service (PES); or how to be self employed by creating their own business; and others.

Active labor market policies. Matching of skills supply and demand also requires further development of active labor market policies, for example, by involving regional-level stakeholders in labor market monitoring and developing public–private partnerships. Selective active labor market policies should focus on serving discouraged workers and people with disabilities and aim to increase female labor force participation by building job-relevant skills that employers demand. Innovation should be encouraged by increasing access to quality tertiary education for motivated TVET graduates, as this route ensures that higher education graduates also possess skills valued in the market.

Evidence-based decision-making. Strengthened central capacity to train, plan, gather, and handle labor market data is urgently needed through support to key organizations such as the National Scientific Center for Employment and Labor Protection. This should include assistance in the preparation of modularized labor market monitoring and management training materials and delivery of the training, as well as learning from international good practices (such as collaboration with recognized international workforce development agencies).

Lifelong learning. Additional demand-side proposals relate to the recognition of Uzbek qualifications, as well as recognition of lifelong learning and work-based learning, both within and outside the country. There is an urgent need to strengthen assessment processes and opportunities for individuals to receive better recognized certification of their actual competencies.

Institutional-level initiatives. Weaknesses in quality of programs should be addressed through adoption of a competency-based, modularized training approach combined with development of the OCS and upgrading of curricula and curriculum materials to meet the changing needs of the labor market. These should be linked to new quality assurance and job certification initiatives for both CVET and iVET programs, as well as to capacity building for management and teaching personnel of TVET institutions, and PES offices. Upgrading of facilities and equipment should be in line with development of curricula and delivery, perhaps with the establishment of centers of excellence as models for the system. TVET institution advisory boards should be established to support institutional activities such as marketing of the institution and its services, piloting of new structures, involvement of worker organizations and local industry, improved training of trainers, involvement in curriculum development, and monitoring of the institution, and others.

Individual-level initiatives. A social marketing campaign should be linked to a new curriculum for CEG to permit informed decision-making for students and parents on routes into and within the labor market. This could be linked to a parallel campaign to increase the prestige of TVET training and increase the involvement of the private sector in training. Training provision for vulnerable groups must be strengthened to ensure inclusiveness of skills development, including support for girls to enroll in TVET programs in nontraditional occupational areas. Focused support should be provided for a program to increase the employability of people from vulnerable groups, and to strengthen and expand the current program promoting self-employment through entrepreneurship development for selected TVET graduates.

I. Introduction

A. Purpose and Scope

1. This sector assessment examines the technical and vocational education and training (TVET) sector in Uzbekistan. It has been prepared as part of the Asian Development Bank (ADB) technical assistance project called Skills Strategies for Industrial Modernization and Inclusive Growth.[1] In Uzbekistan, the public sector largely finances and delivers TVET. There is a small private sector, mostly focused on low-level qualifications such as English and other languages, information technology (IT), and accounting. All TVET institutions (professional schools and professional colleges) are overseen by the Ministry of Higher and Secondary Specialized Education (MHSSE). The sector consists of three types of institutes: (i) TVET colleges overseen by MHSSE only; (ii) TVET colleges jointly overseen by MHSSE and individual sector ministries or companies (e.g., Ministry of Agriculture, Uzbekistan Airways); and (iii) professional training centers overseen by the Ministry of Employment and Labour Relations (MOELR).

2. Recent and ongoing government reforms are changing the Uzbekistan TVET system. Policy guidelines have been issued via decrees and these are currently being developed and interpreted into strategies and actions for the future. The focus of this assessment is on documenting the possible ways forward for the government and the private sector to work together to create a modern TVET system in Uzbekistan. Additional material is included to summarize the impact of the coronavirus disease (COVID-19) pandemic on the economy and on TVET.

B. Methodology and Structure

3. The assessment is based on analysis of secondary data received from government ministries and agencies, as well as reports and documents. The data analysis was complemented by workshops, focus group discussions, and an employer survey. Field trips to Navoi, Andijan, and Angren districts of the Tashkent region allowed local-level interactions with employers, TVET officials, and local government employees.[2]

4. The structure of this sector assessment is as follows. The introductory section sets out the economic context in which the TVET system operates and recent reforms in the sector, including the impact of COVID-19 and the acceleration toward Industry 4.0. Section II briefly describes the education sector, with a focus on the TVET sector's access and enrollment trends. It also examines the financial resources available to the sector and analyzes sector management and governance. Section III focuses on quality issues and learning outcomes, while identifying some challenges and opportunities for the Uzbek TVET system. Section IV considers the sector from the points of view of supply and demand as related to labor market outcomes.

---

[1] Asian Development Bank (ADB). Uzbekistan: Skills Strategies for Industrial Modernization and Inclusive Growth. https://www.adb.org/projects/50025-001/main.

[2] ADB. Forthcoming. *Skills Needs Assessment for Micro and Small Enterprises in Uzbekistan: Enterprise Survey Report.* Manila: Prepared for TA 9256-UZB: Skills Strategies for Industrial Modernization and Inclusive Growth. Manila.

Section V suggests some options for how to improve the relevance and quality of TVET in Uzbekistan based on international best practices and local knowledge. Section VI briefly considers development partner assistance, and section VII concludes the report.

C. Economic Context and Recent Developments

5. **Economic context.** Uzbekistan is a lower-middle-income country with a population of 34.32 million. Its national strategy aims to further reform, structurally transform, and diversify the economy. It has set the ambitious goal of reaching upper-middle-income status by 2030. To achieve this, Uzbekistan needs to transform its current commodity-dependent economy into a competitive, industrialized one. The Government of Uzbekistan has, therefore, launched a development agenda to achieve rapid and broad-based economic growth through economic diversification, industrial modernization, and infrastructure development.[3] Anticipating and addressing labor market challenges has become a government priority, with an increase of more than 30% in the working age population projected by 2030. Although official employment figures show a decrease in unemployment rates (7.5% in 2016[4] and 5.2% in 2018[5]), Uzbekistan is one of the youngest countries in Asia, with almost 60% of the population under the age of 30, and will require a high rate of job creation and well-functioning labor markets to absorb this economically active and growing population. Uzbekistan ranked 105th on the Human Development Index in 2017.[6] Table 1 provides a summary of relevant macroeconomic and social indicators.

6. Successive government industrial modernization policies (2011–2015 and 2015–2019) have outlined key economic objectives, including targets for growth in gross domestic product (GDP), expanding the share of industry value added in GDP, rehabilitating roads, and increasing access to utilities for rural populations. The government's strategy seeks to expand the middle class, promote shared prosperity, and eliminate poverty through the creation of quality jobs for its citizens.

Table 1: Macroeconomic and Social Indicators

Indicator	Year	Value
Proportion of population living below the national poverty line (%)	2018	11.4
Unemployment rate (%)	2019	5.9
Volume of remittances in United States dollars as a proportion of total gross domestic product (%)	2018	15.1
Per capita gross national income, Atlas method ($)	2018	2,020.0
Annual growth rate of gross domestic product (%)	2019	5.8
Life expectancy at birth (years)	2017	71.4
Expected years of schooling (years)	2020	11

Sources: United Nations Development Programme. About Uzbekistan; and ADB. Basic Statistics 2020.

7. **The impact of the COVID-19 pandemic** has been and will remain far-reaching for the foreseeable future. Initial crisis responses that included quarantine "lockdowns," school and workplace closures, social distancing, return migration, and others have been superseded with stronger strategic measures. In a recent

---

[3] Government of Uzbekistan. 2015. *About the Program of Structural Reforms, Modernization and Diversification of Industry for 2015–2019*. Resolution of the President of the Republic of Uzbekistan. No. UP-4707. Tashkent.
[4] ADB. 2018. *Basic Statistics 2018*. Manila.
[5] ADB. 2019. *Basic Statistics 2019*. Manila.
[6] United Nations Development Programme. 2018. *Human Development Indices 2018*.

regional online event, it was stated that Central Asian economies, including Uzbekistan, are recovering from the earlier shocks of the pandemic: migration and remittances are returning to 2019 levels and labor markets are recovering, with fewer work disruptions.[7]

8. With the exception of 2020, when GDP dipped to 1.6%, Uzbekistan's economic growth rate has been relatively stable despite the shocks of COVID-19. In 2019, growth was 5.8% compared with 5.4% in 2018, and has been estimated to rise to 6.2% in 2021 and 5.6% in 2022.[8] For the first three quarters of 2021, real GDP growth in Uzbekistan was 6.9%, and the volume of industrial production increased by 9%, agriculture by 4.2%, construction by 4.5%, and investments in fixed assets by 5%. The production volume of consumer goods for the period increased by 10.9% (food products by 18.3% and nonfood products by 6.9%). Retail turnover for this period increased by 9.8% on the back of financial incentives, the recovery of economic processes in the private sector, and the growth of external economic relations given the main trading partners' economies being stabilized. The volume of loans allocated by commercial banks to the economy increased by 33% compared with the same period last year, and the number of car loans increased by 160% and microloans by 230%. However, recovery of economic activity in some sectors will take longer to reach the prepandemic levels: vehicle manufacture decreased by 32.4% against the first three quarters of 2020, and domestic and foreign tourism, transport, and catering have not yet reached the levels of 2019.[9]

9. Uzbekistan's skills development system faces several challenges and is not well placed to support the government's economic recovery and modernization agendas. Employers report that inadequate workforce skills pose a significant obstacle to firm growth.[10] Other evidence shows a mismatch between the number of graduates in different fields of study and the number of jobs created. This is particularly true for specialized senior secondary school graduates, but also for higher education graduates.[11] While progress has been made in educational system reform, weaknesses persist, including the fact that TVET institutes often can cater to only a very limited number of professions and are widely dispersed, restricting access by potential students, and often lack modern equipment. The quality of education is also highlighted as a concern.[12] Reforms initiated in June 2017 in both the education sector and the labor market address some of these issues. Implementation mechanisms for these reforms are currently being developed (see para. 13 for details).

10. Micro and small enterprises (MSEs), which are defined as firms with up to 200 employees are estimated to represent more than 99% of all enterprises in Uzbekistan and provide employment to more than 77% of all workers in the country.[13] The focus of the technical assistance (TA) is on addressing skills needs in these enterprises targeted to three geographic areas of the country: Angren district of the Tashkent region, Andijan region, and Navoi region which account for about 14% of all MSEs in Uzbekistan.[14] These three geographic areas were selected because (i) they are classified as economic free zones or special economic areas; (ii) MSEs

---

[7] World Bank. 2021. *Overcoming the Pandemic and Ending Poverty in Central Asia.* World Bank regional online event on 16 October 2021: https://kun.uz/en/news/2021/10/16/world-bank-experts-name-key-factors-for-reducing-poverty-in-central-asia (accessed 22 October 2021).
[8] World Bank. Data. GDP Growth (Annual %) – Uzbekistan. https://data.worldbank.org/indicator/NY.GDP.MKTP.KD.ZG?locations=UZ (accessed 23 October 2021).
[9] KUN.UZ. 2021. Uzbekistan's Real GDP Growth Amounts to 6.9% in Jan-Sept 2021. Uzbekistan Central Bank Press Release. https://kun.uz/en/news/2021/10/21/uzbekistans-real-gdp-growth-amounts-to-69-in-jan-sept-2021 (accessed 22 October 2021).
[10] M.I. Ajwad et al. 2014. *The Skills Road: Skills for Employability in Uzbekistan.* Washington, DC: World Bank.; and footnote 2.
[11] World Bank. 2014. *Uzbekistan: Modernizing Tertiary Education.* Washington, DC.
[12] M. Bjarnason et al. 2013. *Private Sector Development Policy Handbook: Developing Skills in Central Asia through Better Vocational Education and Training Systems.* Paris. Organisation for Economic Co-operation and Development (OECD).
[13] Uzbekistan generally classifies the size of enterprises differently from the standard international classification: micro enterprises are defined as 1–20 employees, small enterprises as 21–100 employees, and large enterprises as more than 100 employees. However, the Uzbek classification differs across industry sectors, where small enterprises in some economic sectors can have up to 200 employees. At the same time, the Uzbek classification does not identify medium-sized enterprises.
[14] Information from the Uzbekistan State Committee for Statistics.

contribute significantly to gross regional product in these three geographic areas (66% in Andijan, 37.6% in Navoi, and 57.1% in Tashkent) (footnote 10); and (iii) the government has identified them as the key areas for industrial modernization and job creation. The needs of MSEs differ sharply from those of large enterprises. In addition, they have greater challenges in identifying skills needs and they train employees up to 50% less than large firms.[15] The extent of the skills mismatch for smaller enterprises has become apparent from the results of the employer survey that was carried out in February 2018. A separate report has been prepared on the survey, but some aspects and opinions, especially those related to public–private partnerships (PPPs), are discussed in this report.

11. Uzbekistan's labor market has gender gaps, and the number of economically active women remains considerably lower than the number of economically active men. Although women make up 49.6% of the population, women's share of formal employment is at 45.7% against 54.3% for men. The labor market displays clear gender patterns, with women predominating in lower-paid social sector jobs (in education, health care, social services, accommodation, catering), and men predominating in technical and other more profitable fields (construction, industry, transport, communications, information technology). Women in rural areas are much less competitive in the labor market; they are more likely to work in family-based businesses such as farming or handicrafts due to the limited number of formal sector jobs available locally and, often, their lack of necessary education, qualifications, and skills. Because women spend about as much time on the unpaid domestic tasks that come with their social roles as men do on productive paid work, women have fewer options to work in formal jobs or start their own businesses.[16] Similarly, unemployment rates in Uzbekistan show distinct gender patterns, and the official unemployment rate for women has consistently been higher than for men. There is some indication that women are not seeking jobs at the same rate as men, or at least, are not using official channels for assistance. Unemployed women generally spend more time looking for jobs than men and, on average, remain unemployed for more than a year.[17]

12. The private sector plays a key role in the economy, contributing almost 57% of GDP in 2016. The mechanisms and extent to which the private sector can participate in policy dialogue is currently being investigated in greater detail. For example, in the TVET and higher education subsectors, initial indications show that direct involvement in curriculum development is concentrated in some subsectors only; occupational competency standards appear to be industry-defined in some areas and not in others.

13. **Recent developments.** The basis for Uzbekistan's medium-term strategic planning is the Presidential Decree on Development Strategy for Uzbekistan 2017–2021,[18] which has been further elaborated in the National Action Strategy on Five Development Priority Areas 2017–2021.[19] This 5-year strategic plan is based on five pillars.[20] It is further linked to achieving the Sustainable Development Goals (SDGs) pillars 3, 4, and 5, and the corresponding SDGs of quality education (SDG 4), decent work and economic growth (SDG 8), and reduced inequalities (SDG 10) are directing the reforms in the education sector. The goals of Pillar 4 are relevant to the TVET sector:

4.1: Consistent increase in real income and job creation
4.2: Improving the social security system and health care, improving the sociopolitical activity of women

---

[15] OECD. 2014. *Skills Development in SMEs*. Paris.
[16] ADB. 2018. *Uzbekistan Country Gender Assessment Update*. Manila.
[17] ADB. 2014. *Uzbekistan Country Gender Assessment*. Manila.
[18] Presidential Decree No. UP-4707 (footnote 3).
[19] Government of Uzbekistan. 2017. *Presidential Decree. On the Strategy of Actions on Further Development of the Republic of Uzbekistan for 2017–2021*. No. UP-4947. 7 February. Tashkent.
[20] Pillar 1: Improving the system of state and public construction; Pillar 2: Ensuring the rule of law and further reforming of the judicial system; Pillar 3: Realizing economic development and liberalization; Pillar 4: Developing the social area; Pillar 5: Developing the field of security, inter-ethnic harmony and religious tolerance, as well as the implementation of balanced, mutually beneficial, and constructive foreign policy.

4.3: Implementation of targeted programs to build affordable housing, development and modernization of road transport, engineering, communications, and social infrastructure, ensuring the improvement of living conditions of the population
4.4: Development of education and science
4.5: Improving the state youth policy

14. A new national strategy for 2020–2026 was approved in January 2022.[21] The themes relevant to the TVET sector in the 2017–2021 strategy are also prioritized and strengthened in the new strategy; details are summarized in the Box. In 2022, funding for implementation is covered under the state budget, the national fund for reconstruction and development, funds of executing agencies and banks, and loans and grants from international donor funding agencies. Two bodies have been established to manage the strategy: the Republican Commission for the Implementation of the Development Strategy of the New Uzbekistan for 2022–2026 and a working group.

15. Some of the new decrees and resolutions adopted by the current administration are related to skills development for the labor market. Similarly, a recent presidential decree has put the issue of skills development in the forefront of MOELR and MHSSE and their related institutes.[22]

16. MOELR has established four databases in the past 4 years, of which two are relevant: (i) a database that tracks TVET graduates and their employment now transferred under MHSSE (prof-talim.edu.uz); and (ii) a database of job vacancies (ish2.mehnat.uz). The first of these databases tracks graduates for 3 years in line with the initiative to support young, new graduates in finding a job. The database of job vacancies is used to display vacancies across local employment service centers. This database is not directly linked to a mediation (or job-match) system, but can be used to search for vacancies in specific occupations by local job brokers.

17. In early 2018, several new policy reforms were initiated in the TVET sector, including a presidential order[23] related to improvement of the TVET sector, and a presidential resolution[24] detailing implementation procedures. The presidential order establishes a Republican Commission for the coordination of further improvement of the TVET system and territorial working groups mandated to oversee and feed into the policy changes. Briefly, the order outlines the new TVET policy directions as follows:
(i) subordination of professional colleges under various ministries and agencies, economic associations, commercial banks, and large enterprises;
(ii) alignment of TVET programs with the International Standard Classification of Education;
(iii) establishment of a national qualifications framework aligned with international qualifications frameworks;
(iv) foundation of TVET qualifications on task analysis of actual jobs (the basis for setting occupational competency standards);
(v) new funding modalities for professional colleges; and
(vi) admission to TVET from academic year (AY) 2019/2020 will require graduation from grade 11, will be voluntary, and will be for courses ranging between 6 months and 2 years in length (all pedagogy-related courses will be 2 years).

---

[21] Government of Uzbekistan. 2022. *Presidential Decree. On the Development Strategy of the New Uzbekistan for 2022–2026.* No. UP-60. 28 January. Tashkent. https://lex.uz/docs/5841077 (accessed 17 February 2022).
[22] Government of Uzbekistan. 2017. *Presidential Decree. On Creation of the Republican Commission on Development of Concept of Further Development of System of Secondary Special and Vocational Education.* No. UP-4941. 28 May. Tashkent.
[23] Government of Uzbekistan 2018. *Order of the President. On Measures to Radically Improve the System of General Secondary, Senior Secondary, and Vocational Education.* No. UP-5313. 25 January. Tashkent.
[24] Government of Uzbekistan. 2018. *Resolution of the President. On Improvement of the Activities of the Center of Specialized Secondary and Vocational Education under the Ministry of Higher and Secondary Specialized Education of the Republic of Uzbekistan.* No. PP-3504. 3 February. Tashkent.

Development Strategy of the New Uzbekistan for 2022–2026

The strategy comprises seven key areas:

1. building a humanistic state by raising the honor and dignity of a person and further developing a free civil society;
2. transforming the principles of justice and the rule of law into a fundamental and necessary condition for the development of the country;
3. accelerating development of the national economy and ensuring high growth rates;
4. implementing a fair social policy, developing human capital;
5. ensuring spiritual development and raising this area to a new level;
6. approaching global problems based on national interests; and
7. strengthening the security and defense potential of the country, conducting an open, pragmatic, and active foreign policy.

These areas are divided into 100 goals for 2022–2026. The national program for 2022 is "Year of Ensuring Human Interests and Development of the Mahalla," including 398 measures.

Relevant goals from the new strategy include the following:

- **Goal 37.** Create opportunity for free training in a specific profession for every citizen: double the scale of vocational training; train 1 million unemployed citizens and raise the participation of nonstate educational institutions in this process to 30%. The 2022 program includes state assistance to acquire at least one profession by graduates of general education schools who wish to learn a profession, and recruitment of about 100 foreign teachers to the "Welcome to Jobs" monocenters.
- **Goal 46.** Raise the higher education enrollment rate to 50% and improve the quality of education; raise the level of participation in higher education of youth in 2022 to 38%; raise the admission rate to at least 250,000 students by 2026.
- **Goal 66.** Form an effective system of support for persons with disabilities (PWDs) to improve their quality of life and standard of living: ensure the employment of 12,000 PWDs in 2022; provide benefits to vocational education institutions for vocational and entrepreneurial training of PWDs.
- **Goal 69.** Support women and further increase their activity in society: provide comprehensive assistance in training, mastering professional skills, and provide women with decent work; support women's entrepreneurship; and others.
- **Goal 70.** Improve the state youth policy: provide affordable and high-quality education for young people; create conditions for development of inclusive education in the regions, employment and employment of youth, and development of youth entrepreneurship.
- **Goal 85.** Create new jobs, increase the income of the population and thereby reduce poverty by at least 50% by the end of 2026; help citizens legalize their employment; reduce the unemployment rate among women by 50%, by training more than 700,000 unemployed women and girls; develop and financially support handicraft activity using apprenticeship approaches; and others.
- **Goal 86.** Train at least 300,000 citizens pre-migration in professions and foreign languages; systematize and accelerate measures to issue them with international certificates confirming professional qualifications; reintegrate labor migration returnees, including providing them with employment, improving professional qualifications, and stimulating entrepreneurial initiatives; ensure effective implementation of the project "Investing in Your Future"; and others.
- **Goal 97.** Accession to the World Trade Organization and deepen integration processes with the Eurasian Economic Union.

Source: Government of Uzbekistan. 2022. *Presidential Decree. On the Development Strategy of the New Uzbekistan for 2022–2026.* No. UP-60. 28 January.

18. A recent decree has further developed point (vi) and established a 3-tier TVET system to deliver training programs for basic and advanced occupations (see para. 38 for details).[25]

19. A key strategy of government interventions to increase employment, particularly of graduates from technical and vocational education colleges and specialized secondary schools, is to promote entrepreneurship in addition to other youth employment initiatives. In this respect, there is a general understanding of a need to enhance the development of skills and skills monitoring systems. However, at present, there also appears to be a mismatch between the demand for and supply of skills. Existing classifications of trades and professions are mainly based on educational attainment, and, while some occupations are based on occupational competency standards, many are not.[26] The process of identifying skill sets for developing curricula for professional training programs differs across occupations; for example, the oil and gas industry appears to adhere to a system of job and task functional analysis as in Organisation for Economic Co-operation and Development (OECD) countries. However, most occupations do not have occupational competency standards as defined internationally. A clear system, encompassing all occupations, for defining skills requirements in line with occupational competency standards, tasks, and activities is essential to support industrial modernization and the development of a broader entrepreneurial sector.

20. The relatively new online systems for tracking vacancies and to provide employment services nationwide are currently being merged to streamline information about graduate employability with the public employment services (PES) and with information on private sector companies and institutions. It may be possible to link these databases with an occupational skills monitoring system. Currently, only large enterprises are required to register on the vacancies database, while MSEs are registered on a voluntary basis (two district employment offices estimated about 25% of local MSEs are captured). Interventions to further encourage and support registration of MSEs are being investigated to broaden the range of skill sets in the monitoring system.

21. The Uzbekistan national qualification framework (NQF) was approved on 15 May 2020.[27] It is linked to an educational qualifications framework and an occupational competency standards framework. Initiatives in this area are ongoing and progress has been made in laying the foundation for further developing the occupational competency standards under the responsibility of MOELR and MHSSE. For example, a joint program with Erasmus+ produced a draft sector qualifications framework (SQF) for the information technology (IT) sector in 2019.[28] The current status of the SQF is unknown. The document does not contain specific references to the skills requirements of Industry 4.0 (see para. 28). A recent workshop held by MOELR; MHSSE; the United Nations Educational, Scientific, and Cultural Organization (UNESCO); and the European Union (EU) considered the requirements for further development of the SQF in agriculture (rural development).[29] Although substantial initiatives have been initiated by government and development partners, models have been created and useful lessons have been learned, there remains a clear need for additional inputs to the fledgling systems, as well as support for nationwide application.

---

[25] Government of Uzbekistan. 2019. *Resolution of the President. Additional Measures to Further Improve the Vocational Education System.* No. UP-5812. 6 September. Tashkent.

[26] Ministry of Employment and Labour Relations of the Republic of Uzbekistan. 2015. *Classifier of the Basic Positions of Employees and Occupations of Workers (as Revised in 2015).* A. Navotny, A. Saidov, and R. Baizhumanov (compilers). Tashkent.

[27] Government of Uzbekistan. 2020. Resolution of the Cabinet of Ministers. *On National System of Development of Professional Skills, Knowledge and Competences and the National Qualification Framework of Uzbekistan.* No. 287. 15 May. Tashkent. https://www.ruecvet.uz/en/national-qualifications-framework-of-uzbekistan-is-approved/ (accessed 23 October 2021).

[28] Erasmus+ Nursling. 2019. *Sectorial Qualification Framework of RUz on Information and Communication Technology.* https://ec.europa.eu/programmes/erasmus-plus/project-result-content/946b8e52-88d4-4ba8-93b1-bbe77ac84f8f/Guidelines_SQF_ICT_RUz_en.pdf (accessed 22 October 2021).

[29] UNESCO. 2021. *Education and Labor Market Cooperation in Training of Competitive Employees.* Seminar held on 16-17 September 2021. https://en.unesco.org/news/education-and-labor-market-cooperation-training-competitive-employees-international-seminar (accessed 23 October 2021).

22. The radical changes to the Uzbekistan education system mean that recent trends in enrollments and development during the past decade are less relevant than they might be in terms of forecasting new directions and requirements, especially in the vocational and other secondary and tertiary education levels. Thus, this assessment focuses on future issues, rather than trying to analyze past trends. Some background is, however, useful for benchmarking the system. An Education Sector Plan (ESP, 2013–2017) was published in 2013.[30] The document defines the priority strategic development goals of the education system, based on the principle of lifelong education, and proposes outcomes and outputs for the sector, as well as providing brief action plans for each subsector. However, "experience from 2012–2017 has further shown that following the development and adoption of the ESP it was never really used as a working document . . . there was no follow-up and/or assessment of interim targets."[31] In May 2018, the process for development of an education sector plan for 2018–2022 was launched jointly by the government and the local education group and has resulted in the current ESP for 2018–2022.

23. The government has instituted a number of policies in response to the COVID-19 pandemic. The main thrust of economic development continues to be the enhancement of economic growth and reduction of poverty. There are no significant changes to the prioritization of economic sectors, but the cross-sector importance of IT has increased: government initiatives in the field of IT have been accelerated and enhanced to meet the challenges raised by the pandemic. The Digital Uzbekistan 2030 program was launched in 2017. It provides a road map to strengthen general digital literacy, and addresses digitalization in the fields of construction, energy, agriculture and water management, transport, geology, land registry, health care, education, and other priority sectors of the economy. In reaction to the pandemic, 2020 was declared the Year of Development of Science, Education and the Digital Economy.[32] In relation to this, the President highlighted the need to complete the development of the Digital Uzbekistan 2030 Program in an address to the Uzbek Parliament.[33]

24. These initiatives support the moves toward remote and hybrid forms of working and training, as well as the increasing reliance of industry and commerce on IT solutions and recognizes the dearth of IT specialists (in 2016, only 1.6% of total employment was in IT-related professions, and in recognition of this, the 2019 project "One Million Uzbek Coders" was launched together with the United Arab Emirates). The development of the digital economy is primarily dependent on the availability of IT personnel with high-quality training and education. Highly qualified IT specialists are needed on the delivery side, but the general consumer must also have an ever-increasing ability to use digital services, so digital literacy levels must rise. At the same time, progression to cyber-physical production systems and technologically advanced environments (Industry 4.0, see para. 28) requires systematic training of IT users in all areas of the economy.

25. As elsewhere in the world, the COVID-19 pandemic's initial effect on Uzbekistan's industry and business was widespread shutdowns (85% of small businesses may have been temporarily closed), followed by layoffs and unemployment as companies become increasingly constrained in liquidity and ability to pay taxes (Uzbekistan collected 11% less taxes during the first quarter of 2020).[34] By mid-2020, over 60,000 economic migrants had returned to Uzbekistan, with subsequent loss of remittances, exacerbating unemployment and further straining social services. Loss of export markets resulted from border closures, and domestic production suffered, and continues to suffer from lack of raw materials and components. Young people have been particularly affected,

---

[30] UNICEF. 2013. *Education Sector Plan for 2013–2017*. Tashkent.
[31] UNICEF. 2018. *Developing the Education Sector Plan (ESP) 2018–2022 of Uzbekistan: Situation Analysis of the Education Sector in Uzbekistan*. Tashkent.
[32] Government of Uzbekistan. 2020. *Presidential Decree. On the State Programme for the Implementation of the Action Strategy for the Five Priority Areas of Development of the Republic of Uzbekistan in 2017–2021 in the "Year of Development of Science, Education and the Digital Economy."* No. UP-5953. 2 March. Tashkent.
[33] Address by the President of the Republic of Uzbekistan Shavkat Mirziyoyev to the Oliy Majlis. https://uza.uz/ru/politics/poslanie-prezidenta-respubliki-uzbekistan-shavkata-mirziyeev-25-01-2020.
[34] ADB. *2020. Summary Assessment of Damage and Needs – Annex to the COVID-19 Emergency Response Project (RRP UZB 54282-001)*. Manila.

from both institutional closures and lack of employment opportunities. Measures were instituted to support remote learning, but low-capacity broadband networks and lack of IT equipment have weakened efforts to provide quality remote learning. Broadcast lessons have been available since the early days of the pandemic, but initial content quality was considered poor, and efforts have been made to strengthen the offerings. Remote learning also created discipline problems (student attendance for online or broadcast lessons, and other problems), which further reduced the quality of learning outcomes. General education institutions were reopened in September 2020, and TVET institutions have been reopened for normal face-to-face learning and new intakes since September 2021.

26. Prior to the pandemic, there was a clear trend of lower reliance on the primary agriculture-related sectors and an increase in the importance of the manufacturing and service sectors. The sector structure of the economy continues to change: the share of industry as a percentage of GDP rose from 22.2% in 2017 to 30.0 in 2019 while, during the same period, the share of agriculture, forestry, and fisheries fell from 34.0% to 28.1%, construction rose slightly from 5.7% to 6.4%, and services fell from 38.1% to 35.5%. In 2020, 12 leading industries were implementing modernization and competitiveness programs.[35] Changes in Uzbekistan's priority sectors resulting from recovery plans mainly focus on strengthening industrial competitiveness and increasing energy efficiency.[36] In terms of the government's subsequent project financed by ADB (Skills Development for a Modern Economy Project), there seems to be no reason to revise the thrust of the project in the selected fields for support. However, in view of the much more rapid than anticipated increases in the cross-sector application of IT, it would be wise to reassess the IT sector needs and their impact on the delivery of IT modules by the TVET institutions. The accelerated application of cyber-physical production systems' approaches to manufacture (moves toward Industry 4.0, see para. 28) is also a reason for reassessing IT training programs and their delivery.

27. Recovery strategies can be leveraged to accelerate the greening of economies to promote climate-resilience and sustainability through investment in structural transformations and technological innovations. Such strategies can have "vast job creation potential." Uzbekistan has developed a new industrial policy strategy focused on energy efficiency as one of its priorities for economic recovery. There are also green measures in the recovery plans for the agriculture sector; the recovery plans for the water, sanitation, and hygiene sector; accelerated environmental plans; incorporation of water-related measures in COVID-19 responses; and in all international support of COVID-19 response initiatives (footnote 37).

28. **Industry 4.0.** The fourth industrial revolution (4IR or Industry 4.0) is a term coined to describe the new concepts in manufacturing as supported by innovative technologies such as the Internet of Things, cloud computing, augmented reality, robotics, big data, and others. The ultimate goal of 4IR is the "smart factory"—with fully automated manufacturing processes that use cyber-physical production systems to communicate with each other and with external networks to achieve the common goal.[37] In Uzbekistan, manufacturing contributed only 9% of GDP in 2012 and must increase to 22% of GDP by 2030 to achieve government economic development goals. Such expansion of the manufacturing base offers opportunities to "leapfrog" toward 4IR through a reindustrialization process that will provide improved process performance and higher work quality leading to

---

[35] European Training Foundation. 2021. *Torino Process 2018-2020. Uzbekistan.* National Report. https://openspace.etf.europa.eu/sites/default/files/2021-03/TRPreport_2020_Uzbekistan_EN.pdf (accessed 21 October 2021).
[36] OECD. 2021. *OECD Policy Responses to COVID-19. COVID-19 and Greening the Economies of Eastern Europe, the Caucasus and Central Asia.* https://www.oecd.org/coronavirus/policy-responses/covid-19-and-greening-the-economies-of-eastern-europe-the-caucasus-and-central-asia-40f4d34f/ (accessed 10 October 2021).
[37] I. Kambarov et al. 2019. *The Path to Industry 4.0. Creation of Learning Factory for Education Students of Technical Universities in Uzbekistan.* International Seminar of "NIT, Gifu College" and Partner Universities – Environmental Sustainability, Disaster Prevention and Reduction, and Engineering Education. Gifu, Japan. 17–18 January. https://www.researchgate.net/publication/329585033 (accessed 13 October 2021).

increased production quality and technological content.[38] Though some of the technologies are already in use, there is no current, systematic approach to identifying implementation requirements, and development methods and models for implementing smart production.[39]

29. Mirzaliev et al. have considered the impact of 4IR on the Uzbek job market and the increased need for higher-level science, technology, engineering, and mathematics (STEM) training.[40] They consider coverage of the population with STEM higher education institutions an important factor in the risk analysis of potential discrepancy between supply and demand in the job market resulting from the recent technological advances. They identify a number of research questions that should be addressed, including identification of the key 4IR features shaping the local job market; the key parameters governing education responsiveness to job market changes; the key 4IR features that need to be developed in the local education system to raise the new generation of highly skilled workforce in line with this next industrial revolution. Kambarov et al. (footnote 38) propose that new skills and knowledge are required for workers and students to manage the technological advances and the interdisciplinary and holistic approaches of 4IR. They propose for Uzbekistan the application of the "learning factory" model, which has been shown elsewhere to be an effective tool for developing competence in manufacturing training and education and identify five fields of action: horizontal integration, digital end-to-end engineering, automation, vertical integration, and cyber-physical production systems.[41]

30. A recent ADB-supported survey of the readiness to move toward 4IR has revealed that companies in the Uzbek construction sector and textiles sector (the two sectors included in the survey) consider digital or information and communication technology (ICT) skills as well as creative thinking and design skills (and, to some extent, adaptive learning skills) will become the most important skill areas in the next 5 years.[42] In a global survey by McKinsey,[43] of the advanced cognitive skills, project management, critical thinking, and decision-making were prioritized; and of the technological skills, basic digital upskilling was the main priority, followed by advanced IT skills and programming. In any case, in the face of globalization and increasingly competitive markets, Uzbek companies will need to adopt reskilling and upskilling strategies and support the processes of lifelong learning. These divergent views emphasize the importance of inputs into training planning from the industry sector skills councils (SSCs). Curriculum planning clearly needs to consider a training approach that provides noncognitive metaskills or different types of skill sets rather than focusing on individual skills.

31. The ADB-supported survey also considered the supply of 4IR-ready workers from the perspective of training institutions and notes that only about one-third of the institutions offer courses relevant to the implementation of 4IR, and the vast majority of institutions would need financial support and additional capacity building to be able to develop and deliver relevant programs.

---

[38] I. Kambarov et al. 2018. *Uzbekistan towards Industry 4.0. Defining the Gaps between Current Manufacturing Systems and Industry 4.0.* https://www.researchgate.net/publication/329557969 (accessed 12 October 2021).
[39] Footnote 38.
[40] S. Mirzaliev et al. 2021. Aspects of Non-Profit STEM Education System Creation for Industry 4.0 in Uzbekistan. *Journal of Hunan University (Natural Sciences).* 48 (10). https://johuns.net/index.php/publishing/164.pdf (accessed 10 October 2021).
[41] U. Wagner et al. 2012. The State-of-the-Art and Prospects of Learning Factories. *Procedia CRIP.* 3 (2012). pp. 109–114.
[42] ADB. 2021. Assessing Implications of Industry 4.0 on Jobs and Skills in High-Growth Industries in Central Asia. Draft presentation: Survey report is forthcoming.
[43] McKinsey & Company. 2021. *COVID-19: Implications for Business.* https://www.mckinsey.com/business-functions/risk-and-resilience/our-insights/covid-19-implications-for-business?cid=other-eml-alt-mip-mck&hdpid=5ab42177-02f8-4862-a8e7-f49e87b330f9&hctky=1693897&hlkid=e497f81dfe9b4fb99c8993de60b86564 (accessed 21 October 2021).

32. **Future of work and TVET.** The World Economic Forum 2020 considered that preparation for the future of work will require innovation (in ways of upskilling and reskilling), equality of opportunities, digitalization and sustainability (as related to climate change, social and economic sustainability).[44] According to the OECD, the future of work in the post-pandemic world will have a focus on equality of opportunities (young people have been disproportionately affected by the COVID-19 crisis), digitalization (impacting home and hybrid working, as well as the displacement of jobs), continuous lifelong learning (incorporating reskilling and upskilling, keeping skills relevant in a changing world), the "gig" economy (i.e., more individuals working on short-term or freelancer contracts), and individual well-being (as related to the quality of jobs and redesign of functions).[45] Implementation of 4IR approaches and solutions have accelerated beyond all expectations. Companies have met the challenges in a variety of ways, with a strong focus on workforce development.

33. A survey of civil society organizations in Uzbekistan found that the organizations' responses to COVID-19 focused on the use of digital learning tools (virtual classroom software such as Teams, Google classroom, Moodle, and synchronous video communication tools such as Zoom, Telegram, WhatsApp, Facebook Live). The organizations' beneficiary groups had changed in response to the difference of the impact of COVID-19 on different population groups: youth programs had increased by 62% and women's programs by 54%, reflecting that recovery plans must acknowledge the need for equality of opportunity.[46]

34. Already before the onset of COVID-19, the Government of Uzbekistan has continued to reform legislation related to skills development and labor market. A decree recognizing the International Standard Classification of Education (ISCED) and aligning Uzbekistan's qualifications with the International Standard Classification of Occupations (ISCO-08) was promulgated in late 2019 (footnote 27). The education law of 1997 was replaced with a new law to cover all types of education—formal, informal, and lifelong learning.[47] A major government initiative was the legislation to permit the creation of sector skills councils in 29 sectors and their subsectors.[48]

35. From the perspective of formal TVET, it is imperative that graduates are equipped with skill sets that not only meet current needs of the labor market, but also provide analytical and creative competencies and the ability to learn and adapt to new industrial paradigms and technological advances as they arise. Uzbekistan has recently issued several decrees and resolutions to support this approach as part of its recovery plans. Looking to the future requirements of higher-level learning, the status of several colleges has been raised from the status of teaching at Uzbekistan NQF levels 3 and 4 to the level of *technikum*, teaching at Uzbekistan NQF levels 4 and 5.[49] Entrance exams for the professional colleges under line ministries and new *technikums* were held in November 2021. To support those affected most by the pandemic and to strengthen practical or industrial training students will receive a stipend (from budgetary sources) during such training.[50]

---

[44] S. Y. Lim. 2021. Presentation on Smart Teaching to Prepare Students for the Digital World, referring to weforum.org/projects/future-of-work. Singapore Institute of Technical Education. https://drive.google.com/drive/folders/1ouATQ8gOINsd0Wsp6wfg1Ni5TGBy1T33?usp=sharing (accessed 2021).
[45] OECD. The Future of Work. https://www.oecd.org/future-of-work/#a-world-reshaped-by-digitalisation (accessed 2021).
[46] N. Ergashev et al. 2021. Civil Society Organisations and Human Capital Development: Uzbekistan Country Report (Draft of 4 February 2021). European Training Foundation. https://openspace.etf.europa.eu/resources/civil-society-organisations-and-human-capital-development-uzbekistan-country-report (accessed 20 October 2021).
[47] Government of Uzbekistan. 2020. *Law of the Republic of Uzbekistan on Education*. No. ZRU-637. 23 September. Tashkent.
[48] Government of Uzbekistan. 2020. Resolution of the President. *On Measures for Cardinal Improvement of the Qualifications Assessment System and Providing the Labor Market with Qualified Staff*. No. PP-4939. 31 December. Tashkent.
[49] Government of Uzbekistan. 2021. Resolution of the President. *On Measures to Strengthen the Relationship of the Educational Process between Higher, Secondary Specialized and Professional Education Institutions, as well as Industrial Practice with Industry Organizations*. No. PP-5241. 31 August. Tashkent.
[50] Government of Uzbekistan. 2021. Resolution of the Cabinet of Ministers. *On Additional Measures to Support Young People in Need of Social Protection*. No. 616. 4 October. Tashkent.

36. As mentioned in para. 21, work has been continuing on the establishment of the Uzbekistan NQF, as well as on the expansion of industry bodies to support the definition of professional standards and assessment procedures, and others. In the future, attestation of industrial training masters will be based on the new professional standards.[51] The commercial and industry sectors are progressively contributing to development of these standards. In connection with this, the cabinet of ministers recently approved the regulations for the new qualification centers and industry councils.[52]

37. In the continuing vocational education and training (CVET) field, individual correspondents have reported that there currently appears to be some competition between MOELR's professional training centers (PTCs) and the programs offered by professional colleges. The MOELR PTCs that offer retraining services are free to participants and the programs are based on practical WorldSkills approaches, whereas professional college programs are fee-paying and tend to be more academic. The role of MOELR has been greatly expanded under recent presidential resolutions.[53,54] Resolution 4804 confirms the establishment of 16 Welcome to Job (Isghga Markhamat) monocenters as well as 138 PTCs for the inhabitants of *mahallas*. The later resolution (5140) establishes a further 28 PTCs and, in 864 *mahallas*, 1,000 vocational training points for basic qualifications in sewing, culinary and confectionery, hairdressing (male and female), computer literacy, the basics of accounting and entrepreneurship, and other simple areas. The resolution also defines the responsibilities of the *khokimyat* and MOELR for implementation, as well as the sources of funding for investments and running costs of the PTCs and vocational training points. However, the aim is for PTCs gradually to become self-financing.

---

[51] Government of Uzbekistan. 2021. Resolution of the Cabinet of Ministers. *On Measures to Improve the Procedures for Attestation of Pedagogical Personnel of Organizations of Preschool, General Secondary, Secondary Specialized, Vocational and Out-of-School Education*. No. 572. 17 September. Tashkent.

[52] Government of Uzbekistan. 2021. Resolution of the Cabinet of Ministers. *On Additional Measures to Further Improve the System for the Development of Professional Skills and Knowledge*. No. 616. 30 September. Tashkent.

[53] Government of Uzbekistan. 2020. Resolution of the President. *On Additional Measures Aimed at Attracting Entrepreneurship, Increasing Labor Activity and Vocational Training of Poor and Unemployed Citizens, as well as Ensuring Employment of the Population*. No. PP-4804. 11 August 2020. Tashkent.

[54] Government of Uzbekistan. 2020. Resolution of the President. *On Measures to Further Improve the System of Training for Working Professions*. No. PP-5140. 8 June 2021. Tashkent.

II. The Uzbekistan Education Sector

A. Structure of the Education Sector

38. The legal basis for provision of education in Uzbekistan is currently Article 72 of the Republican Constitution and the Law of the Republic of Uzbekistan on Education adopted in September 2020 (footnote 48), together with various resolutions and decrees. The document continues the policy of free and compulsory education, and there is a new focus on the issues of educational quality. The recent United Nations Children's Fund (UNICEF) situation analysis indicates that the following general issues are covered by the new law:

   (i) stronger focus on realization of inclusive education;
   (ii) addition of lifelong education and health education;
   (iii) independence of the private sector;
   (iv) independence of higher education institutions (HEIs); and
   (v) requirement for centralized data gathering from universities, to ensure reliability, validity, and comparability of data.

39. Figure 1 indicates the current organizations involved in administration and delivery of education. The Ministry of Preschool Education (MOPSE) was only recently established, and its organizational structure is not yet complete. The dashed lines indicate proposed lines of responsibility that are awaiting approval. For example, the Department for Vocational Education used to be an autonomous institution, but is now subordinated as a department of the Ministry of Higher and Secondary Specialized Education (MHSSE), and its restructuring is ongoing.

40. The umbrella organization for the education sector is the Cabinet of Ministers, which has a department for social sectors development. The Ministry of Finance (MOF) is responsible for financing systems, while the Ministry of Economic Development and Poverty Reduction is responsible for demographic projections, forecasting demand, developing admission programs to educational institutions, planning for material and technical inputs into the education system, planning for government grants, and others. MOPSE is responsible for early childhood education and MHSSE for higher education and TVET. The Ministry of Employment and Labour Relations (MOELR) is responsible for individual retraining programs and for employee training (continuing vocational training) at the professional training centers (PTCs).

41. The Ministry of Public Education is responsible for general education schools and out-of-school educational institutions, as well as for some higher education institutions and institutes of advanced teacher training. It comprises the central ministry headquarters in Tashkent, as well as regional departments and district/city departments, which provide administrative and methodological support to the educational institutions in their subordinated territories. Until 2007, funding of educational institutions was also carried out through these departments, but currently, funding is through the territorial subdivisions of the MOF.

Figure 1: Organizational Structure of the Uzbekistan Education System, 2022

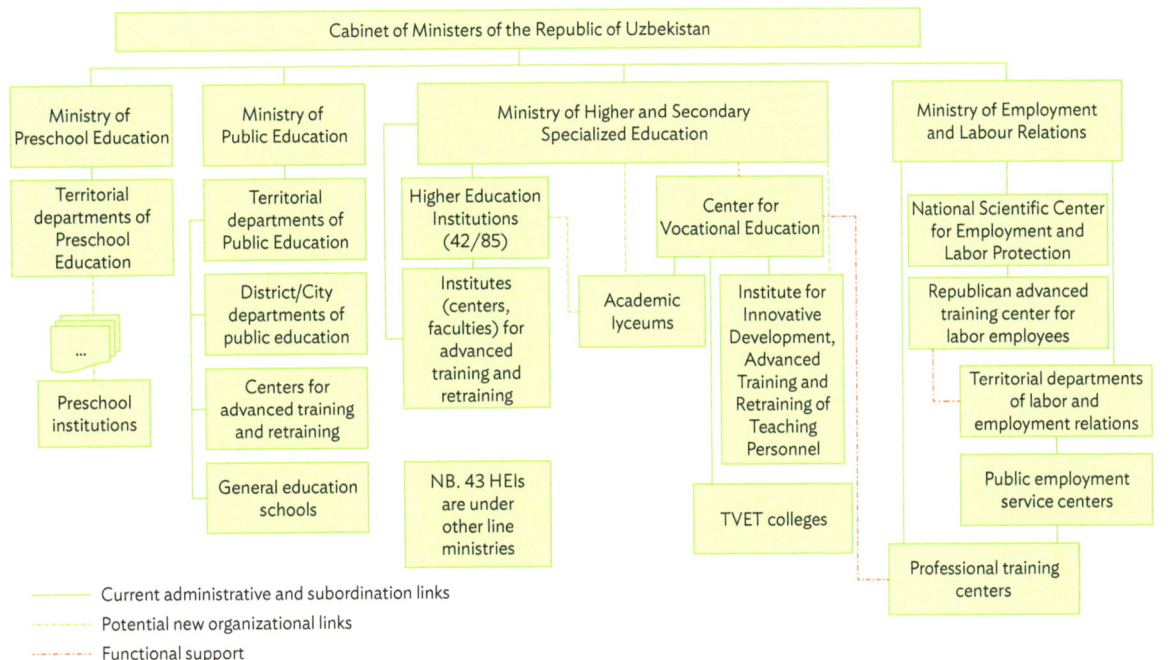

HEI = higher education institution, TVET = technical and vocational education and training.
Source: Authors' interpretation of various decrees.

42. MHSSE is responsible for 42 of the 85 HEIs, academic lyceums (secondary specialized education) and professional colleges.[55] Its organization differs for higher education institutions (directly under the central ministry headquarters in Tashkent, with no intermediaries), and specialized secondary and vocational education institutions which fall under the regional departments of MHSSE. In 2019, the former Center for Secondary Specialized Vocational Education (CSSVE) which carried the responsibilities for curriculum development and methodological support to the academic lyceums and professional colleges as well as to the PTCs under MOELR was disbanded and its roles and responsibility subsumed within MHSSE.

43. From 1997 to 2017, Uzbekistan operated a 12-year general education system involving 4 years of primary education and 5 years of general secondary education, followed by 3 years in a TVET college or academic lyceum. Graduates of TVET colleges and academic lyceums were then eligible to enter higher education. According to a recent report, about 10% of TVET and academic lyceum graduates entered higher education, of which 70% were graduates of academic lyceums and 30% were graduates of TVET colleges.[56] From academic year (AY) 2017/2018, this system was changed to an 11-year general education system, involving 4 years of primary education, and two cycles of secondary education of 5 years and 2 years each. Currently, the government is rapidly increasing the number of places in HEIs to meet the high demand for university places that the reform has generated. In AY2020/2021, about 1.8 million applicants participated in the HEI entrance exams, competing for about 165,000 places (see also para. 62).

44. It was initially intended that the education in grades 10 and 11 would ensure that all graduates from general education had received a basic professional skill through 1,540 newly established school production and training units (UPKs). This professional training delivery system effectively replaced the former compulsory TVET college

---

[55] Government of Uzbekistan. 2019. *Education Sector Plan (ESP) of Uzbekistan 2019–2023*. Tashkent.
[56] UNICEF. 2018. *Developing the Education Sector Plan 2018–2022 of Uzbekistan: Situation Analysis of the Education Sector in Uzbekistan*. Tashkent.

education so that all TVET college programs are now elective, with entry after completion of either grade 9 or grade 11. However, from 2019, the UPKs have been discontinued. Grade 9 graduates who wish to pursue TVET will now be able to enroll in professional (initial vocational education and training [iVET]) schools (budget-funded for 2-year programs), which will provide both academic and technical programs. On graduation, they will be able to apply for (fee-paying) courses in professional colleges or *technikums,* apply to a higher education institution (HEI), or enter the labor market. Pupils who elect to stay in general secondary schools will graduate after grade 11 and can elect to enter the labor market or proceed to a *technikum* for technical training or apply for entry to an HEI.

45. The structure of the Uzbekistan education system from AY2019/2020 is in Figure 2. There is a 3-year interim period during which the old structure is phasing out and the new structure is phased in.

Figure 2: Uzbekistan Education Structure from Academic Year 2019/2020

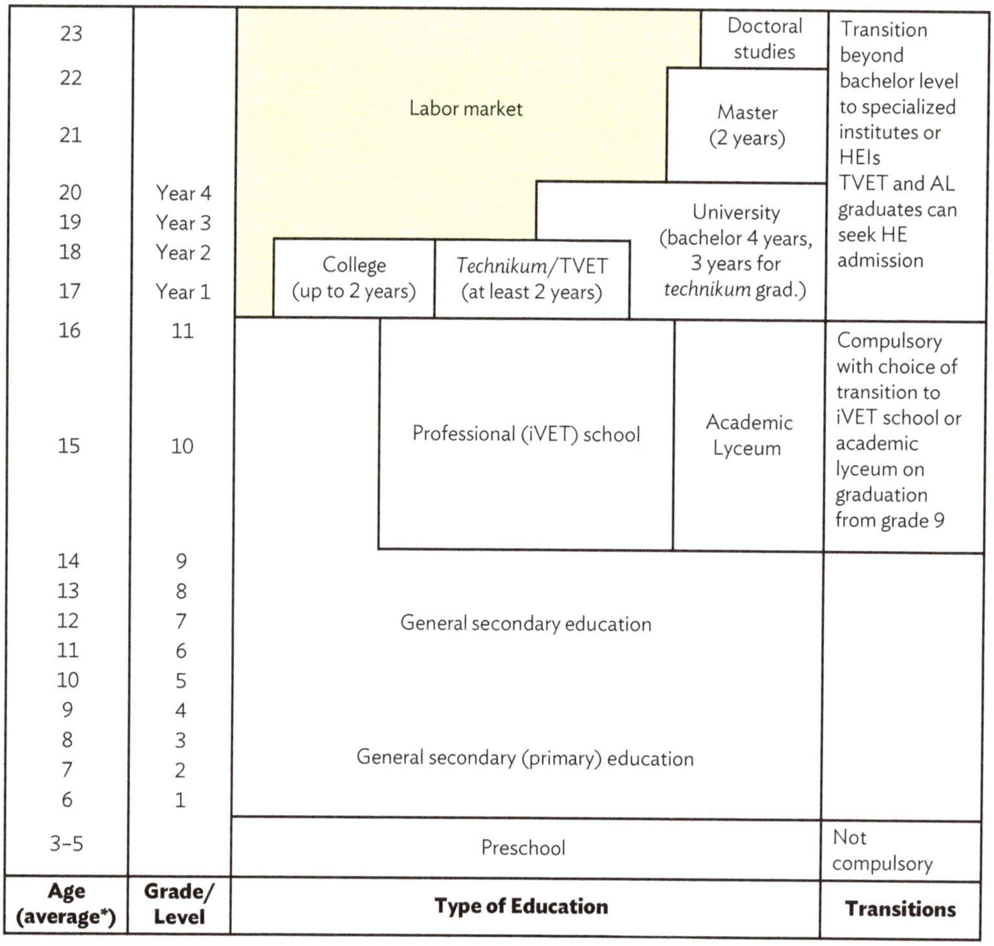

Age (average*)	Grade/Level	Type of Education				Transitions
23		Labor market			Doctoral studies	Transition beyond bachelor level to specialized institutes or HEIs
22					Master (2 years)	
21						
20	Year 4				University (bachelor 4 years, 3 years for *technikum* grad.)	TVET and AL graduates can seek HE admission
19	Year 3					
18	Year 2		College (up to 2 years)	*Technikum*/TVET (at least 2 years)		
17	Year 1					
16	11					Compulsory with choice of transition to iVET school or academic lyceum on graduation from grade 9
15	10	Professional (iVET) school			Academic Lyceum	
14	9	General secondary education				
13	8					
12	7					
11	6					
10	5					
9	4					
8	3	General secondary (primary) education				
7	2					
6	1					
3–5		Preschool				Not compulsory

AL = academic lyceum, HE = higher education, HEI = higher education institution, iVET = initial vocational education and training, TVET = technical and vocational education and training.

* Children can begin school when parents decide to enroll them. The normal age range is 6–7 years old, and 6 years is taken here as the average grade, entry age.

Note: Academic year (AY) 2017/2018 and AY2018/2019 were transition years where the structure allows for some degree of choice for pupils to follow the "old" system or the "new" one.

B. Education Enrollments: Overview

46. Enrollments in upper secondary education (grades 10, 11, and academic lyceum) or TVET have fallen since the beginning of the century, but are expected to begin rising rapidly. This is clearly a reflection of the reduced population growth around the turn of the century (see Figure 3 and Table 5). Extrapolation of current population figures using the average population growth rate of 2.8% (2000–2017) shows that enrollments in general secondary, specialized secondary, and professional education from 6- to 17-year-olds will increase by 36% by 2030.[57] This increase in enrollments will have many consequences for the education system. At the same time, the number of 18-year-olds entering either higher education or the labor market will increase by about 20% by 2030.

47. Uzbekistan does not collect data on gross and net enrollments, partly because the entry age to formal education is fluid. However, enrollment rates are clearly high (Table 2).

Table 2: Enrollment Rates by Age and Gender in Formal Education, Academic Year 2017/2018

Age Group	Males (%)	Females (%)	Total (%)
15 years old	96.1	95.7	95.9
16 years old	93.5	94.5	94.0
17 years old	92.4	92.6	92.5

Source: Authors' calculations based on data from the State Statistics Committee.

48. The impact of the recent reforms on general education (increasing from 9 years to 11 years) was immense in AY2017/2018 and AY2018/2019, including significant changes in gender ratios (Table 3). What the future holds for the TVET system in terms of enrollments is currently unclear, as the entire system is moving from a supply-side system providing 3-year programs of general and professional subjects, regardless of the real skills requirements of the professional field to a demand-driven system based on elective TVET programs.[58]

Table 3: Enrollments in Grades 10 and 11, Academic Year 2018/2019

	Number of Students in Grade 10	Girls	Number of Students in Grade 11	Girls
Total	456,397 (95.5% of 15-year-olds)	49.3% (97.0% of 15-year-old girls)	279,788 (57.5% of 16-year-olds)	52.2% (60.0% of 16-year-old girls)

Source: Ministry of Higher and Secondary Specialized Education.

49. Table 4 shows the number of students who attended some type of formal education and/or training in the most recent academic years to give an indication of the different types of education channels available to Uzbekistan citizens.

C. Secondary General Education (Grades 10–11)

50. Until AY2017/2018, pupils graduated from general secondary education at grade 9 and entered specialized secondary education either at TVET colleges or at academic lyceums for 3 years. Generally, TVET and academic lyceum graduates either entered the labor market or proceeded to higher education.[59] General subjects

---

[57] Authors' calculations based on State Statistics Committee population data.
[58] Based on discussions with senior officials from the Ministry of Public Education in January 2018.
[59] Total AY2015/2016 graduates from academic lyceums could have accounted for only about 59% of AY2016/2017 enrollments in higher education (there were 36,100 academic lyceum graduates in 2016). The skills survey indicates very low rates of employment for these graduates, but some do enter the labor market and do not continue to higher education. Up to 4.8% of AY2015/2016 TVET graduates accounted for 41% of HEI enrollments that year (assuming no other sources of entrants than the previous year's academic lyceum and TVET college graduates).

Table 4: Number of Students by Type of Education
('000)

Institution/Academic Year	2012/2013	2013/2014	2014/2015	2015/2016	2016/2017
Preschool	549.8	575.8	620.8	634.1	691
General education (Grades 1–12)	4,491.0	4,489.7	4,539.7	4,670.7	4,825.0
Academic lyceums	112.0	111.9	108.5	103.7	101.3
TVET colleges	1,573.9	1,515.0	1,450.0	1,394.9	1,358.1
Higher education institutions	258.3	259.3	261.3	264.3	268.3
Institute of senior research associates	1.2	1.2	1.0	1.4	1.4
Persons trained and adding qualifications at enterprises and organizations	295.0	294.9	278.2	293.1	268.6
Barkamol Avlod children's centers	96.2	102.7	105.3	112.3	116.6
Schools of music and art	47.8	49.0	52.8	58.1	72.4
Sports education establishments	349.3	366.7	350.1	362.4	368.7
Total	**7,774.5**	**7,766.2**	**7,768.4**	**7,601.9**	**7,802.8**

TVET = technical and vocational education and training.
Source: State Statistics Committee.

formed the bulk of the TVET curriculum in grades 10 and 11, with professional subjects being introduced in grade 11 and continuing into grade 12, so both TVET and academic lyceum students de facto received almost 11 years of general education.

51. The interim system from AY2017/2018 was intended to ensure that all graduates from general education would receive a basic professional skill through UPKs, but this system is now discontinued.[60] From AY2020/2021, grade 9 completers may continue their compulsory education in grades 10 and 11,[61] or move to a professional school for 2 years of combined academic and trades training, or move to an academic lyceum. Each of the 73 academic lyceums remaining after the reorganization will be attached to a university[62] (with university lecturers providing some of the teaching), though academic lyceum graduates will neither be required to enter the affiliate university, nor will they be guaranteed a university place (each university has its own entrance exam and entry requirements).

52. The system reform introduced from AY2020/2021 gives grade 11 graduates (including professional school graduates, and adults who can show 2 years of equivalent lifelong learning) three choices for transition:
 (i) direct entry to the labor market based on their general education diploma;
 (ii) progression to a *technikum* or a multiprofile professional college for either deeper study in their chosen field or to select and train for a new profession through programs that will range from 6 months to 2 years

---

[60] The professional field depended on either the programs offered by the local TVET college UPK (at 1,046 colleges) or, in the case of remote schools, one of the 50 basic programs provided by the UPKs established at each of 484 remote schools. Students attend school for 34 weeks a year, and they received 6 hours a week of theory and practice in the profession of choice, starting in grade 10 (total of 408 hours of instruction). The private sector (employers) were involved through contributions to the curriculum development process (as well as through provision of work experience or internship places). Each student had the opportunity for 36 hours of work experience at the end of grade 10 and, again, at the end of grade 11. With this qualification (referred to as a "junior" qualification, but could also be a full qualification depending on the field), grade 11 graduates could choose one of the three transitions: to work, to go a TVET college, or take entrance exams for HEI.
[61] Note: 76% of students who graduated in 2017 chose to continue to grade 10 and 96% of grade 9 students who graduated in 2018 chose to remain in general education.
[62] An additional four academic lyceums are military-based under the jurisdiction of the Ministry of Defense and there is one national, specialized music and art lyceum.

in duration, depending on the field (the *technikums* and professional colleges conduct entrance testing/examinations); and

(iii) progression through the entrance examinations process to a university or other higher education institution.

D. Transition to Technical and Vocational Education and Training

53. During 2000–2018, the population of Uzbekistan rose over 30% to 32.66 million, with an average population growth rate of 2.8% over that period. However, population growth has been uneven for different age groups over the same period; for example, the 0–21 age group grew by only 1.2%, and the 0–18 age group decreased by 2.4% with consequent reductions in enrollments in education. Figure 3 shows the population distribution for the resident population.

54. **Demand increasing.** Table 5 simplifies the population data to show that the earlier trend in population decline related to the target age groups has turned to a net population increase.

55. From AY2011/2012 to AY2015/2016, there was an increase of 7.4% in the number of pupils in general education (grades 1–9). In the same period, enrollments in grade 1 rose by 26.3% from 507,400 to

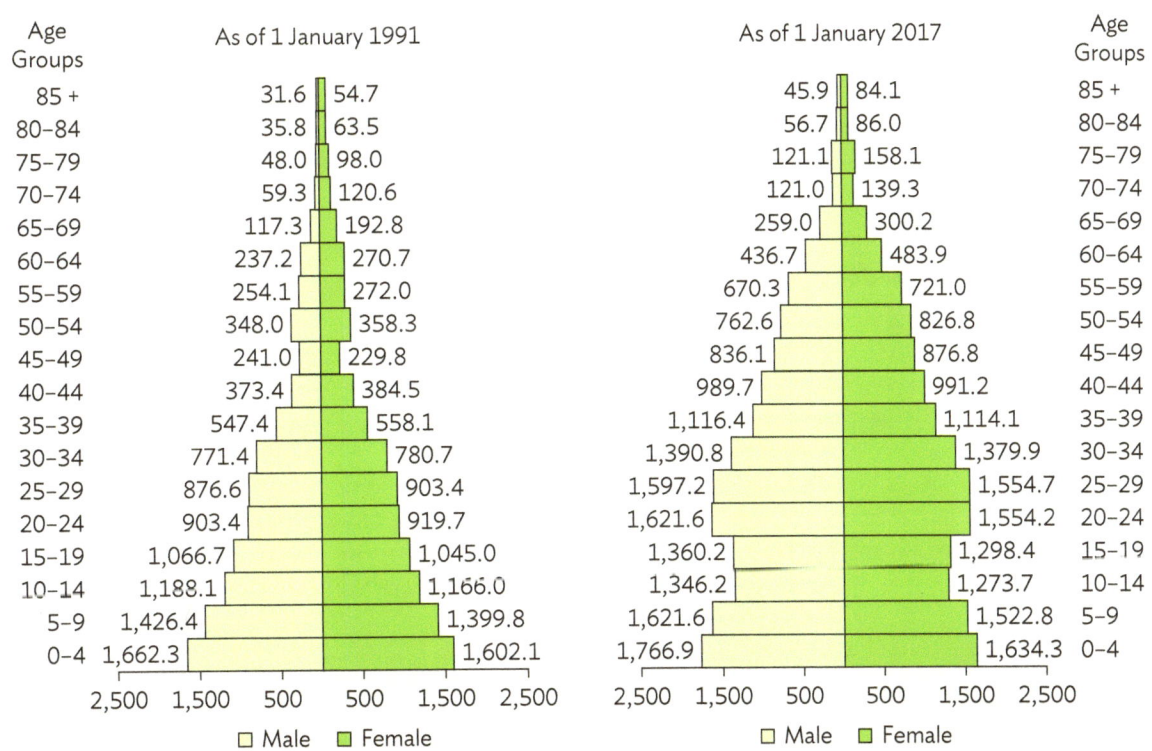

Figure 3: Age Composition of Resident Population of Uzbekistan ('000)

Source: State Statistics Committee.

640,600 pupils, but the graduation rate from grade 9 dropped by 14.8% (from 558,000 to 475,300 pupils). This indicates quite a high rate of repetition, but also a high rate of retention up to grade 9 (Table 6). Recent data for the policy transition years (2017–2019) indicate that there has been a 2.7% dropout or retention rate (1.8% for girls and 3.6% for boys) between grades 10 and 11.

56. Admissions to TVET have declined steadily since 2012/2013, Table 7a illustrates that the number of TVET students declined by 13.7% during 2012/2013–2016/2017. Similar trends, though lower rates of decline, can

Table 5: Population Change, by Age Group, 2000–2017

Age Group	2000			2017			% Change		
	Total	Male	Female	Total	Male	Female	Total	Male	Female
0–21 years	12.9	6.6	6.4	13.1	6.8	6.3	+1.2	+2.51	−0.2
0–18 years	11.5	5.9	5.7	11.2	5.8	5.4	−2.4	−1.1	−3.8
<1 year	0.5	0.3	0.3	0.7	0.4	0.3	+30.7	+32.6	+28.7
2 years	0.5	0.3	0.3	0.7	0.4	0.3	+32.3	+34.5	+30.1
3 years	0.6	0.3	0.3	0.7	0.4	0.3	+18.5	+20.0	+16.9

Note: As of 1 January (inhabitants, millions), totals may differ due to rounding up or down.
Source: Authors' calculations based on State Statistics Committee data.

Table 6: Admissions to and Graduation from General Education, Academic Years from 2011/2012 to 2015/2016

	2011/2012	2012/2013	2013/2014	2014/2015	2015/2016	Change %
Number of general education pupils	4,491,000	4,489,700	4,539,700	4,670,700	4,825,000	7.4
Number of admissions to grade 1	507,400	534,000	582,500	622,500	640,600	26.3
Graduation after grade 9	558,000	533,000	500,200	482,600	475,300	−14.8
% Change in admissions	N/A	5.2	9.1	6.9	2.9	N/A
% Change in graduations	N/A	−4.5	−6.2	−3.5	−1.5	N/A

N/A = not applicable.
Source: Authors' calculations based on State Statistics Committee data.

Table 7a: Enrollments, Admissions, and Graduations, Technical and Vocational Education and Training Colleges, Academic Years from 2012/2013 to 2016/2017

	2012/2013	2013/2014	2014/2015	2015/2016	2016/2017	Change %
TVET college students (end of year)	1,573,900	1,515,000	1,450,700	1,394,000	1,358,100	−13.7
TVET college admissions	515,100	496,100	468,800	451,800	446,400	−13.3
Graduations from TVET colleges	518,800	505,500	498,100	482,200	478,400	−7.8
% Change in admissions	N/A	−3.7	−5.5	−3.6	−1.2	
% Change in graduations	N/A	−2.6	−1.5	−3.2	−0.8	

N/A = not applicable, TVET = technical and vocational education and training.
Source: Authors' calculations based on State Statistics Committee data.

be seen in the data for academic lyceums. Table 7b illustrates the complex situation resulting from the system reforms; the decline in TVET enrollments and graduations continued to AY2019/2020 as admissions to TVET were suspended. After AY2017/2018, TVET institutions began to be differentiated into professional schools, professional colleges, and *technikums*, with final introduction of the reforms and recommencement of admissions from 2020 (see para. 52). This has led to an upturn in the admissions to TVET, but it is still too early to perceive trends.

57. Table 8 shows the number of students graduating from grade 9 compared with the number of admissions to TVET, academic lyceums, and higher education. The reduced graduation from grade 9 is directly reflected in the lower admissions to TVET and academic lyceums. Although there is officially no repetition of grades in Uzbek schools, the figures indicate that this is in fact quite high.

58. Pupils enroll in grade 1 at different ages, and this is reflected in the broad range of ages of TVET students, with 5% aged 15 years or less, 30% aged 16 or less, 33% aged 17 years, 30% aged 18, and 3% aged 19 or above.

59. Six languages are used as the medium of instruction in general education (Uzbek, Russian, Karakalpak, Kazakh, Tajik, and Turkmen). In TVET institutions, this is reduced to Uzbek (93%), Russian (4%), Karakalpak (3%), and Tajik (0.2%).

Table 7b: Enrollments, Admissions, and Graduations, Technical and Vocational Education and Training and Academic Lyceum, Academic Years from 2017/2018 to 2020/2021

	2017/2018	2018/2019	2019/2020	2020/2021	2021/2022*	Change %
TVET and AL enrollments	1,163,200	728,100	282,400	229,900		−80.2
TVET and AL admissions	85,836	78,103	43,161	172,941	79,000	+101.5
Graduations from TVET colleges	457,051	454,931	468,809	177,654		−61.1
Graduations from ALs	32,720	31,628	46,453	19,820		−39.4

AL = academic lyceum, TVET = technical and vocational education and training.
*Initial data for TVET only, no details available.
Source: Authors' calculations based on State Statistics Committee. 2021. www.stat.uz/en/official-statistics/social-protection (accessed 12 February 2022).

Table 8: Progression from Grade 9 to Technical and Vocational Education and Training and Academic Lyceums with Higher Education Admissions, from 2011/2012 to 2015/2016

	2011/2012	2012/2013	2013/2014	2014/2015	2015/2016	Change %
Graduations from grade 9	558,000	533,000	500,200	482,600	475,300	−14.8
Admissions to TVET colleges	515,100	496,100	468,800	451,800	446,400	−13.3
Admissions to academic lyceums	38,700	37,700	36,500	34,200	35,100	−9.3
Admissions to TVET and academic lyceums	553,800	533,800	505,300	486,000	481,500	−13.1
Admissions to higher education	63,100	62,300	64,100	63,000	61,200	−3.1

TVET = technical and vocational education and training.
Source: Authors' calculations based on State Statistics Committee data.

E. Technical and Vocational Education and Training Enrollments

60. TVET was established as a separate education sector in Uzbekistan in 2000. The compulsory upper secondary education was split into two streams: TVET for 3 years, leading to a professional qualification and academic lyceums, also for 3 years and focused on preparing students for entry to university, but also providing a professional qualification in a limited number of subjects (e.g., IT sector). In AY2000/2001, enrollments were 30,862 in TVET, 37,336 in academic lyceums, and 166,466 in higher education. This reform was followed by rapid expansion of the education system, and by AY2011/2012, enrollments in TVET had peaked at 1,599,031 students, enrollments in academic lyceums had peaked at 112,876 students, and enrollments in higher education were 253,026 (down from a peak of 278,674 in AY2005/2006). From AY2011/2012 to AY2016/2017, there was a steady decline in the enrollments in TVET. Meanwhile, enrollments in higher education showed a small decline to AY2011/2012, after which enrollments rose gradually (Figure 4).

61. Transition to TVET in AY2017/2018 was impacted by the reintroduction of grade 10 (see Figure 4), with admissions to first year TVET programs dropping by 61%. The effect on admissions to academic lyceums was a reduction of 41.7%. It should be noted that the higher number of girls electing to remain in grade 10 has created a greater gender bias in academic lyceums, which will likely be reflected in enrollments in higher education in future years. The impact on TVET admissions is even bigger than on academic lyceums, with a total reduction of 61.6%. Again, the sum effect has been to create a greater gender gap in the TVET system (from 2.2% in AY2016/2017 to 11% in AY2017/2018).

62. Demand for higher education is very high: in AY2020/2021, over 1.8 million people participated in the university entrance exams, and enrollment was 165,201 (footnote 63). Perceptions seem to be that higher education qualification is in greater demand by employers, and evidence shows that the rate of return on

Figure 4: Trends in Postsecondary Student Enrollments

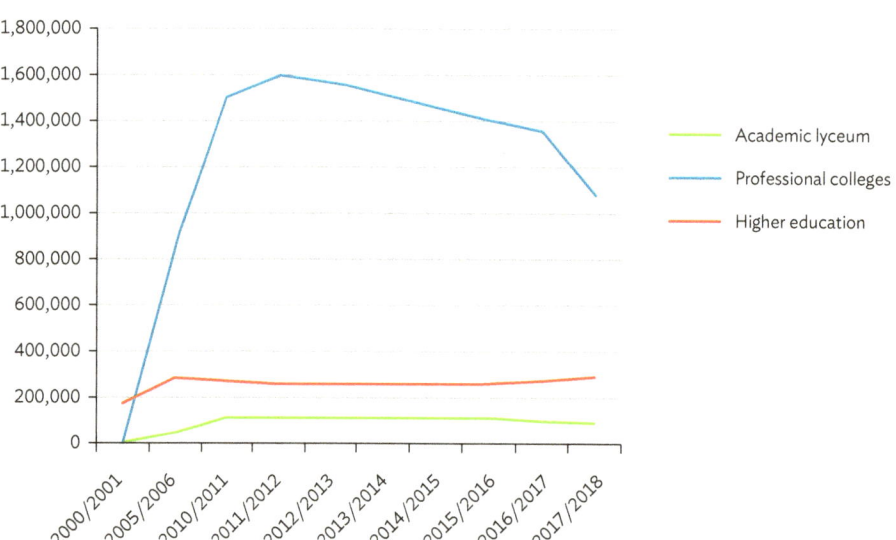

Note: 2000–2009 data not to scale.
Source: State Statistics Committee.

investment is much higher for higher education than for other types of education, including TVET. While the large increase in enrollments is promising (from 85,600—58.72% male and 44.78% female—in AY2017/2018), selection of courses may not be the most effective from the labor market perspective. In AY2019/2020, 48% of HEI students were studying humanities and only 25% study in the production and technical spheres (only 33.4% of students in the STEM subjects were female).

63. Considering the broad reforms, especially those related to the recent expansion of general education from grades 9 to 11 and the new range of continuing education choices open to grade 9 and grade 11 graduates, forecasting of enrollments in TVET over the next decade is extremely difficult. However, some inferences can be made, and some general conclusions can be drawn. Table 9 illustrates one scenario. Pupils graduating from grade 9 from AY2018/2019 onward were still allowed to choose between continuing their education in general secondary grade 10 or entering year 1 of academic lyceum. However, there was no progression from grade 9 to TVET institutions, so there was no admission of year 1 TVET students in either AY2018/2019 or AY2019/2020. Those students who elected to remain in grade 10 during the first years of the reform graduated at the end of AY2018/2019 and AY2019/2020 and would have been eligible to enroll in TVET programs for AY2020/2021. Latest figures show that only 7.3% of them elected to enter professional colleges or *technikums*. Table 9 assumes an arbitrary increase of 10% for AY2021/2022, but until further data are available extended projections are not feasible.[63]

Table 9: Possible Progression Scenario from Grades 9 to 10, Technical and Vocational Educational Institutions, and Academic Lyceums
('000)

	2014/2015	2015/2016	2016/2017	2017/2018	2018/2019	2019/2020	2020/2021	2021/2022
Graduations from grade 9[a]	500,198	482,588	475,324	466,111	475,654	466,395	484,503	539,200
Progression to grade 10			0	0	280,324	454,323	450,654	362,395	224,103
Progression to iVET (from 2020/21)[b]							135,000	148,500
Admissions to professional colleges/ *technikums*[b]		451,980	446,704	171,744	0	0	79,000	86,900
Admissions to academic lyceums[c]		34,192	35,090	20,442	19,820	25,000	25,000	25,000
Admissions to grade 10, TVEIs, and academic lyceums		486,172	481,794	472,510	474,143	475,654	466,395	484,503
Difference		14,026	−794	−2,184	−8,032	0	0	0

iVET = initial vocational education, TVEI = technical and vocational educational institution.
[a] Actual enrollments to academic year (AY) 2020/2021, no allowance for repetition or dropout. Enrollment for AY2021/2022 is the previous grade 5 enrollments in AY2017/2018.
[b] Assuming 10% annual increase in enrollments to iVET schools, professional colleges, and *technikums* from the level of 79,000 in AY2020/2021
[c] Assuming academic lyceum enrollments return to pre-reform levels.
Sources: Data for AY2017/2018 from State Statistics Committee. Authors' calculations and estimates, in italics.

---

[63] In 2021, enrollment of graduates from grade 9 was about 79,000 students into 339 colleges/*technikums*, and about 160,000 students into 555 professional schools and 73 academic lyceums.

64. **Specialization.** Under the current system, each region prepares a 3-year forecast for needed TVET graduates based on demography and economic development. These forecasts are used to determine the number of TVET enrollments for each sector of study. Table 10 shows the distribution of enrollments between the various specializations. These specializations are further broken down into subject spheres and the trends in enrollments by subject spheres are shown in Table 10. As indicated in Figure 4, there has been a general decline in TVET enrollments, which is partly accounted for by the decline in the population of the relevant age groups.

65. The subspecializations of economics, pedagogy, and law have seen steep declines (Table 11). Discussions with senior TVET specialists, employers, and trade organizations indicate that employers are increasingly looking for higher education graduates, especially in the teaching profession, banking, and related economic fields and law. However, it must also be noted that an increase in higher education enrollments is not sufficient to have been responsible for all the reduction in TVET numbers, so the question remains, where have these students gone? Another reason for decline in these fields is a result of the policy of allowing students to select the programs they wish to join. If students are aware of the declining value of a TVET qualification in their chosen field, they may either try to pursue higher education, or select another profession. The extent to which different fields are perceived as "easy" or "difficult" by Uzbek students is a clear area for further study regarding careers education and labor market demand, but is outside the scope of this assessment.

66. Enrollments in social sciences, natural sciences, journalism and information, and art are much more stable, with declining numbers likely reflecting the decline in population rather than changes in required numbers of professionals. The observed steady rises in enrollments in production technology and architecture and construction are anticipated in an economy that is broadening its industrial base. However, the declines in enrollments in computer science and communication technologies require further examination (see section III B). The trends in the health sector are also declining, but this is probably explained by the fact that the health sector has been seen by many families as having greater status (especially for girls, according to some informants); this led to over-enrollment in health-related programs, but the resultant high competition for employment is apparently now having an impact on enrollments.

67. It seems clear that the linking of TVET program quotas to demand as defined by the regional development plans is becoming more sophisticated; large employers have always been part of the process, but discussions with employers indicate that micro and small enterprises (MSEs) are also able to make increasing contributions.

Table 10: Distribution of Students at Technical and Vocational Education and Training Colleges, by Subject Sphere, Academic Year 2016/2017

Subject Sphere	Proportion of Enrollments (%)
Humanitarian sphere	8
Social sphere, economics, and law	11
Industrial and technical sphere	49
Agricultural and water management	11
Health and social care	10
Services	11
Total	**100**

Source: State Statistics Committee.

Table 11: Enrollments in Technical and Vocational Education and Training Colleges by Field of Study, Academic Years from 2011/2012 to 2016/2017

Field of Study/Academic Year	2011/2012	2012/2013	2013/2014	2014/2015	2015/2016*	2016/2017*
Total	**1,599,031**	**1,573,906**	**1,514,988**	**1,450,730**	**1,394,903**	**1,358,064**
Humanitarian sphere	**248,766**	**207,102**	**170,083**	**146,480**	**122,694**	**115,389**
Pedagogy	226,245	181,802	144,691	121,332	97,346	89,962
Social sciences			54	818	913	906
Natural sciences	824	998	1,088	1,111	1,654	1,589
Art	21,697	24,302	24,250	23,219	22,781	22,932
Social sphere, economics, and law	**341,778**	**307,403**	**262,334**	**207,279**	**169,075**	**147,584**
Journalism and information	2,757	3,731	3,769	3,254	2,541	2,437
Economics	297,339	277,751	241,446	192,936	156,619	136,368
Law	41,682	25,921	17,119	11,089	9,915	8,779
Industrial and technical sphere	**619,390**	**669,646**	**690,460**	**694,656**	**676,72**	**664,587**
Engineering	175,169	184,390	190,224	194,746	198,113	199,950
Production technology	202,950	217,969	234,380	233,804	221,858	217,781
Computer and information technology	180,302	192,964	189,261	185,782	170,811	157,418
Architecture and construction	38,442	42,585	45,390	51,813	59,979	64,371
Communication, information, and telecommunication technologies	22,527	31,738	31,205	28,511	25,959	25,067
Agriculture and water management	**111,534**	**125,753**	**142,693**	**147,057**	**140,033**	**144,516**
Agriculture, forestry, and fisheries	19,362	25,552	31,368	35,040	31,601	32,885
Management and farm management	21,833	22,245	24,620	24,275	22,281	23,437
Agro-engineering	53,696	56,475	60,608	62,017	58,870	58,752
Veterinary science	11,157	13,209	15,424	14,518	16,748	18,429
Irrigation and melioration	5,486	8,272	10,673	11,207	10,533	11,013
Health and social care	**159,181**	**144,826**	**127,825**	**132,528**	**146,277**	**137,920**
Health	151,921	139,346	123,463	126,686	143,721	135,824
Social care	7,260	5,480	4,362	5,842	2,556	2,096
Services	**118,382**	**119,176**	**121,593**	**122,730**	**139,835**	**147,798**
Service sector	53,483	54,879	58,071	53,490	70,182	79,552
Transport	62,050	61,306	59,734	64,848	62,940	61,022
Environmental protection	2,849	2,991	3,788	4,392	6,713	7,224

Source: State Statistics Committee.
* Includes some non-distributable data.

68. **Admission procedures**. Up until the reforms, the regional authorities applied a forecasting system to define labor market needs and thereby, college intake numbers, as well as the TVET programs they apply to. Thus, admission levels were derived more or less from the following process by January or February each year:

(i) Companies contact the *khokimyat* and express their need for new employees for the next period.
(ii) The *khokimyat* collates this information from different companies and sends out a description of the overall demand for TVET graduates to the TVET colleges.
(iii) At each TVET college a coordinator prepares an offer to the *khokimyat* specifying how the TVET college can meet the demand.
(iv) The *khokimyat* makes the overall decision and informs the TVET college about how many students they can admit for which programs (the quota).[64]

69. TVET colleges then announced the vacancies and conducted information sessions during "professional orientation" in class 9 (part of the general secondary education formal careers guidance process).

70. It is envisaged that a similar process will be applied to assist the professional colleges to plan their programs and the number of places they will offer for each program. The recent reforms mean that it will be virtually impossible to forecast accurately the demand for places in the TVET system in the short term. Current work on skills needs analysis and establishment of a skills monitoring system will help to alleviate the situation by providing students with relevant skill sets.[65] The new student demand-driven approach also means that the authorities will be able to propose programs for students to choose from, but it is not yet possible to predict how consumers (the students) will react to what is put on offer. Clearly, social marketing of career opportunities is a key need and should be connected to broader careers education and guidance (CEG). Thus, in the light of the change to a student demand-based TVET system, the institutions, especially the *technikums* and the mid-profile professional colleges, will need to market their offerings to prospective students. From AY2019/2020 this will be a difficult process for the colleges as they have no historical data on which to base enrollment projections.

71. There is evidence that some MSEs have participated in this 3-year forecasting process and are comfortable with it. Some companies recruit directly from the TVET colleges and provide any necessary in-company training themselves. However, although employers have been contributing to the planning process, there is a clear desire for more direct cooperation between employers and colleges. Lack of communication between employers and TVET providers is one of the weaknesses of the TVET system; communication should be both directly between employers and local training providers as well as on a higher system level. These issues are further discussed in section V (A and C).

72. As an example of direct communication between companies and business, 80 staff from a new factory being established in a free economic zone (FEZ) were first trained for 1 month at a TVET college before being sent abroad for further training. Many of the new companies in FEZs have direct connections with local TVET colleges, with the TVET college providing the theoretical training, while companies provide practical training.

73. In the light of the new reforms to general secondary education, students will have the opportunity to pursue either further studies or select a profession through joining an elective TVET program. Currently, there is no way to determine the actual demand from grade 11 graduates, so colleges must prepare themselves to become demand-side institutions; they will need to market themselves and their programs to students and parents.

---

[64] The *khokimyat* decision is based on analysis of the offers from the colleges and includes reference to the equipment available at each TVET college. The Ministry of Economic Development and Poverty Reduction is also involved in the process, but this may be restricted to its contribution to the regional development planning process.
[65] Footnote 2.

F. Curriculum

74. From the beginning of AY2020/2021, grade 9 completers will continue in general secondary school or academic lyceum or professional school for 2 more years. On completion, they will have the opportunity to transition to further vocational education and training or to higher education or to the labor market. Except for professional schools, TVET institutes will no longer teach general subjects, and the professional fields will be delivered as programs of 6–24 months in length. The curriculum will be a state curriculum based on CBT principles. Each professional college can adapt up to 15% to regional demands and the adapted curriculum should be approved by the regional TVET branch.

75. The curriculum is expected to be based on the occupational competency standard (OCS). In principle, the OCS is reviewed every 5 years, while the Uzbek curriculum is reviewed every 3 years. However, the current curriculum is based on the classification for each occupation, which sets out the needed knowledge, but which is not usually related to occupational standards based on job functional analyses. The process for curriculum development should preferably include several stages which correspond to the first three stages of the Analysis, Design, Development, Implementation, and Evaluation (ADDIE) model:[66] (i) employers identify requirements through the OCS; (ii) a committee (consisting of TVET teachers and employers) holds workshops to create the curriculum content; (iii) the standards are enhanced in MHSSE; and (iv) course material and assessment procedures are developed. Implementation of the curriculum is currently monitored by a working group, whose members are TVET teachers, representatives from the ministry, and employers.

76. According to the British Council tourism project (under which the sector has been assisted to define the OCS and curriculum for professional tourism colleges and set up a sector skills working group in late 2017 in the Tashkent Tourism College), the planning process at the *khokimyat* and collation of information for the MHSSE curriculum department is ad hoc and currently has no clear lines of responsibility and communication. MHSSE has noted that the curriculum development process should be faster for curricula to match technological developments.

77. In the curriculum implemented until 2017, students had 4 months of internship in companies: 2 months during the second year of their program, and 2 months during the third year of their program. Discussions with sector stakeholders and the results of the employer survey have highlighted that the planning, implementation, and assessment of the internships can be improved. Field visits revealed that it is sometimes unclear what the students are supposed to do during the internship. The period of practice is tracked by a special journal and by the trainee's diary.

78. Three examples of curricula have been examined: "techniques of programming" and "occupational health and safety" from 2016, and "fundamentals of entrepreneurship and business" from 2008.

79. The first two curricula follow the same structure:
   (i) Introduction to the subject
   (ii) Purpose and objectives of the subject
   (iii) Needed knowledge and skills
   (iv) How the subject links to other subjects
   (v) Application of knowledge and pedagogical approach
   (vi) Technical training facilities

---

[66] The ADDIE model of curriculum development is an internationally recognized process invented by Florida State University in 1975. The ADDIE model relies on each stage being done in the given order, but with a focus on reflection and iteration. The current curriculum development process in Uzbekistan corresponds generally to this model with extra steps of approval by higher authories. However, the current evaluation phase is somewhat ad hoc.

(vii) Thematically plan with number of hours
(viii) Content of the themes
(ix) Recommended literature and list of websites

80. The structure can be characterized as an input-oriented curriculum with focus on content and hours spent for each section. In the sections defining knowledge and skills the focus is on knowledge and not on learning objectives; in other words, the focus is on what the student should know rather than on what the student can do.

81. The entrepreneurship curriculum includes an 80-hour program on how to start a business: "fundamentals of entrepreneurship and business" for professional colleges and academic lyceums. The subject is also input-based with a weak formulation of learning objectives. But the division of hours (36 for theory and 44 for practice) as well as the part of "practical seminars, experimental lessons, and themes for independent works" indicate a much more practical pedagogical approach. There are nine overall themes, which follow a logical structure.

82. The curriculum also includes text-based introductions to each of the themes, as well as a long list of recommended literature, laws, and decrees. All in all, the curriculum can be used by the teacher to prepare and implement interesting, motivating, and effective training in entrepreneurship.

83. Continuing vocational education and training (CVET) or upskilling and reskilling is provided through specialized institutions (PTCs) in the form of short courses, particularly aimed at retraining unemployed job seekers, but also providing contract retraining or further training to company employees. The staff of the Korea International Cooperation Agency (KOICA) PTC in Tashkent develop their own shorter curriculum.[67] The difference between the KOICA-style curriculum and the iVET curriculum is that in the latter, the division between theory and practice is 50/50 while the KOICA PTC provides 70% practice and 30% theory.

G. Teaching Staff

84. The teaching staff in initial TVET is divided into two: teachers who teach theory only, and masters who provide or guide practical training in workshops. According to Article 44 of the Law of the Republic of Uzbekistan "On Education," the right to engage in teaching activities is a person with the appropriate education, professional training, and possessing high moral quality. Pedagogical activity in educational institutions is not allowed for people with a criminal record. A pedagogical, engineering–pedagogical, or corresponding higher education in the subjects taught is needed. Theory teachers can come directly from university and teach at a professional college. Those with no pedagogical prerequisites will need extra training from a pedagogical institute.

85. The number of TVET teachers at the end of AY2016/2017 was 119,105. Of these, 86% were teachers and 14% were masters. Among teachers and masters, 49% were women (52% of teachers and 33% of masters). As of 1 August 2019, this number had dropped significantly to 34,187, of whom 65% were teachers and 35% masters.[68] This reflects the drop in TVET enrollments resulting from the reforms. The bigger drop in the number of teachers is caused by many subject teachers being transferred to general education schools as subject teachers. About 73.3% of teachers have a higher education qualification (98% in 2017), and 5.4% have TVET qualification (1% in 2017).

---

[67] KOICA has been supporting the establishment of PTCs for several years; the first fully operational PTC was established in Tashkent and named KOICA PTC.
[68] Data provided by MHSSE.

Teachers are further divided into professional levels as in Table 12. Clearly, more teachers with higher education qualifications have left the TVET system, presumably because they are in higher demand from the general secondary schools than teachers with a TVET qualification.

86. Of the masters, 7.6% have a higher education qualification (70% in 2017), and the remaining 92.4% do not have a degree (30% in 2017). The drastic reduction in the number of highly qualified masters is a serious cause for concern; presumably highly qualified masters have left to work in companies. In 2017, 68% of teachers and masters were younger than 40 years, and a further 20% were under 50 years of age. If many of them have been forced into a career change and have shifted away from TVET and into the commercial sector, it may not be easy to attract them back to TVET once demand increases. Senior TVET officials estimated that before 2017, the expected need for new teachers or masters was about 3% of the total number of pedagogical staff, or about 3,000–5,000 teachers and masters per year.

87. If the rough enrollment projections shown in Table 9 hold firm, the number of teachers and masters in the system would be generally sufficient to achieve reasonable teacher-to-student ratios. However, the actual situation regarding technical specialties may be very different. Table 13 shows the staffing situation in the priority sectors to be supported under the Skills Development for a Modern Economy Project. While the intention of

Table 12: **Professional Levels of Technical and Vocational Education and Training Teachers, 2017 and 2019**

Professional Level	Percentage (%) 2017	Percentage (%) 2019
Chief teacher	2	2
Lead teacher	4	6
Senior teacher	13	14
Teacher with higher education qualification	79	73
Teacher with secondary education qualification	2	5
Total	**100**	**100**

Source: State Statistics Committee.

Table 13: **Technical and Vocational Education and Training Teachers and Masters in Five Priority Sectors, as of 1 August 2019**

Education Fields	Total	Including							
		Teachers					Workshop Masters		
		Higher Senior Teachers	Leading Teachers	Senior Teachers	Teachers with Higher Education Degree	Teachers with TVET Degree	1st Degree	2nd Degree	No Degree
Light industry	1,801	26	70	171	940	95	15	39	445
Service	3,151	24	96	175	1,709	195	23	93	836
ICT	1,692	35	89	186	834	18	14	46	470
Construction	2,211	15	81	191	1,067	92	26	86	653
Agriculture and irrigation	4,127	13	97	333	2,252	164	22	101	1,145
Total SDMEP relevant fields	**12,982**	**113**	**433**	**1,056**	**6,802**	**564**	**100**	**365**	**3,549**

ICT = information and communication technology, SDMEP = Skills Development for a Modern Economy Project, TVET = technical and vocational education and training.
Source: Ministry of Higher and Secondary Specialized Education.

the project is to provide higher levels of training, only 13.1% of the masters in those sectors have a university-level qualification. In addition, recent site visits (in September 2019) indicate that many TVET teachers and masters have left or their employment has been terminated, and colleges are maintaining only administrative and security staff. Further investigation of this issue is required.

88. The age distribution of teachers and masters is outlined in Table 14. As can be seen, teachers and masters are quite young, with 68% being below 40 years of age.

89. Across the regions, the age distribution of the total number of teachers and masters is relatively similar, with Bukhara and Samarkand having quite a high proportion of teachers younger than 30. The overall low age of the teachers is probably because many of them come straight from university and have no or little work experience from companies. This is confirmed by a weighted average age of 36 years and simple average of 14 years of teaching experience.

90. Regarding continuing professional development (CPD), teachers are expected to stay updated. Training programs are designed and delivered by the Institute for Innovative Development, Advanced Training and Retraining of Teaching Personnel of the Vocational Education System. All senior and pedagogical staff must pass courses on upgrading qualifications every 4 years. The duration of direct upgrading is set to at least 4 weeks' equivalent or 144 hours. However, this training does not incorporate real work experience.

Table 14: Age Distribution of Technical and Vocational Education and Training Teachers and Masters, 2017

Age Group	Percentage (%)
Under 30	36
30–39	32
40–49	20
50–59	11
60+	1
Total	**100**

Source: State Statistics Committee.

H. Facilities and Equipment

91. In AY2016/2017, there were 1,422 TVET colleges operating in Uzbekistan, which is up slightly from 1,408 in AY2012/2013. Latest detailed data from AY2015/2016, indicate that 1,044 of these have attached workshops. Total dormitory places are 97,800 (about 9% of total places). The total design capacity of all colleges is 1.04 million students. In terms of facilities, 54% of the total physical area is defined as educational, 20% for teaching and auxiliary purposes, 16% utility buildings, 10% residential, and 1% is for rent. With implementation of the education reform in AY2019/2020, the number of TVET colleges has been reduced to 630, including 340 for professional schools under MHSSE, 147 for midprofile colleges attached to line ministries or industrial groups, and 143 to be *technikums* attached to universities. Of the remaining 809, 30 will be converted to professional training centers providing short reskilling or upskilling courses under MOELR, but most will be converted to other uses.[69] Similarly, the 144 academic lyceums will be reduced to 73, with one academic lyceum attached to each public university.

92. Table 15 indicates the percentage of TVET colleges and enrollments by region in AY2016/2017.[70] The percentage distribution of TVET colleges and students in each region generally correspond, indicating that the average enrollment capacities of the colleges are generally similar. There are, of course, some exceptions to this.

---

[69] Government of Uzbekistan. 2019. Resolution of the President. *Additional Measures to Further Improve the Vocational Education System*. No. UP-5812. 6 September. Tashkent.
[70] Data are not yet available on the distribution after the institute closures effected in AY2017/2018.

93.   Generally, TVET colleges claim to have relatively good facilities and equipment, though this may result from something of a misconception about the definition of "good" equipment and facilities. In visits to Navoi and Andijan, equipment was mentioned as a strength of the TVET system. One assessment of the TVET sector notes that the Government of Uzbekistan invested heavily in building new colleges and academic lyceums, and in equipping these institutes with new textbooks and equipment. At the same time, it notes that, although the progress in developing the TVET system has been impressive, specifically in terms of infrastructure development, further improvements in education and skills quality and governance are needed.[71] The amount of equipment in TVET institutes is also an issue. For example, in AY2016–2017 there was an average of only 33.4 computers per TVET college in the country.

94.   Indeed, a lot of the technical equipment could certainly be improved, and at least some of the mismatch between companies' needs and TVET students' competence levels can be attributed to TVET colleges not having equipment equivalent to that used in the companies. It is likely the case that there is a very diverse level of facilities and equipment across regions and TVET institutes. A lot of equipment is out of date and/or not functioning properly. The impression is that the unsatisfactory state of facilities and equipment is something that is well known, but is not acknowledged publicly. A leading official in a new joint venture vehicle manufacturing project reinforced this point, noting that the industry is working on Industry 4.0 equipment when the colleges might not even have Industry 2.0 equipment.[72]

95.   There also appears to be serious problems with the availability of consumable materials and supplies for the students: a practical cooking class with no ingredients apart from some flour and sugar; welding workshops which are very clean, but with few welding rods or welding materials. The main cause of the shortages is mainly the insufficient budget funds for consumables. The practice has been for the colleges to raise funds by themselves for consumables, but the regulations concerning accountability and transparency were not clear, and college principals reported varying degrees of success in fundraising. Under the recent decree on TVET from February 2018, colleges can retain funds that they raise through contract training and advisory work, and others, to be used for the purchase of training materials and consumables. This is a current practice, but the extent of fundraising and the application of those funds remain unknown without an in-depth study of TVET colleges. Such institution-based fundraising and application should be encouraged through linking the TVET institutions with enterprises, which would help to better design, develop, and regulate the processes to incentivize financial sustainability and the fit of skills training for market needs.

Table 15: Geographic Distribution of Technical and Vocational Education and Training Colleges and Enrollments, Academic Year 2016/2017

Region	Colleges (%)	Enrollments (%)
Tashkent City	8	8
Khorezm	6	6
Ferghana	10	11
Tashkent	8	7
Syrdariya	3	3
Surkhandarya	8	8
Samarkand	11	12
Namangan	8	8
Navoi	3	3
Kashkadarya	9	10
Djizzak	5	4
Bukhara	6	6
Andijan	8	9
Republic of Karakalpakstan	7	5
Total	**100**	**100**

Source: State Statistics Committee.

---

[71] B. Mirkasimov. 2017. *Uzbekistan Skills Mismatch*. Tashkent.
[72] Industry 2.0 refers to the beginning of the 20th century and the start of the second industrial revolution, for which the main contributor was the development of machines running on electrical energy. Industry 4.0 is a name for the current trend of automation and data exchange in manufacturing technologies, including cyber-physical systems, and encompasses digitalization, the Internet of Things, smart factories, and others (see also paras. 28–37).

I. Assessment

96. Teachers and masters assess students using a 5-point system that is standardized nationally. In addition, individual practice classes are evaluated on a 100-point evaluation system. The total score is rounded off to a 5-point system. In the TVET classrooms visited, the journal books for recording of assessments were present. To monitor students' readiness to graduate, current, intermediate, and final assessments are applied. In the final summative assessment, two types of assessment are used: a "diploma work" or thesis to test theoretical knowledge and a practical test. For the practical, employers are involved and, according to the former CSSVE, employers account for 70% of the practical assessment. The results of the final evaluation also depend on the result of the internship and the thesis. However, employers have repeatedly mentioned that the assessment of the internship periods could be improved. Pre-reform, TVET was part of the compulsory education system and so promotion from grade to grade until graduation was, in principle, automatic. Currently, only the 2-year programs of the professional schools (equivalent to grades 10 and 11 of general education) are part of the compulsory requirement for education, whereas professional colleges and *technikums* are entered on a voluntary basis. New assessment systems are being developed based on needed occupational competencies, especially for those participating in CVET programs and certification of existing competencies (footnotes 49 and 52), and it is anticipated that these new procedures will also be standardized for use in the elective professional training institutions.

J. Graduates

97. To track the graduates of the TVET system an address database is set up with weekly monitoring of the employment of graduates under MOELR (http://www.college.mehnat.uz/). The database tracks only whether the graduate is employed and receiving a salary, not whether the graduate is being employed in line with their qualification and/or skills. Table 16 shows graduate placements from TVET colleges at the end of AY2016/2017.

98. Out of the 223,100 employed, 9,900 (20% of graduates and 40% of employed graduates) are employed within the acquired specialty. The information received from the former CSSVE did not say anything about the 46% of graduates who are not "engaged." Therefore, it is not clear whether they are simply not in the database or whether they are unemployed. The information was received in October 2017 (i.e., a few months after graduation), so it may be that many graduates still had not found employment after the summer break. Also, many of the males would be in military service.

Table 16: Technical and Vocational Education and Training Graduate Placements in Academic Year 2016/2017

	Number	Percentage of Graduates (%)
Graduates	456,800	100
No information	210,900	46
Engaged	245,900	54
Of whom		
Employed	223,100	49
Continued to higher education	14,700	3
Engaged in entrepreneurial activity	8,232	2

Source: Ministry of Higher and Secondary Specialized Education.

K. Quality Assurance

99. There is no systematic and comprehensive quality assurance (QA) process in the current TVET system. The overall TVET system has been very centralized and does not give the flexibility for TVET colleges to adapt to local conditions and thereby meet the differential demands of the labor market. The system is more geared toward management of funds and documents than on improving the quality of TVET education and training, and several quality control procedures can be identified.

L. Private Technical and Vocational Education and Training

100. There is a small private TVET sector, which is funded through course fees on a commercial basis. Private providers must register as nongovernment educational institutions. However, courses are generally restricted to foreign languages, computer technology and IT, and economic fields such as accounting, secretarial, and business courses. Data on the volume of this business and the number of graduates and their employability are not currently available.

M. Financial Resources

i. Public Funding and Income Generation

101. Current procedures for the collection and analysis of statistical data in Uzbekistan are not always aligned with international good practice and, thus, standard measures of efficiency in the education sector are not always available. Unless otherwise sourced, the data below was received from the MOF and has these limitations. Expenditures are expressed in absolute Uzbek sum, and are not adjusted to account for fluctuations in inflation or purchasing power parity. Generally, budget allocations equal actual expenditures. As well as budget allocations, the education system also receives nonbudget allocations from discretionary sources for infrastructure investment. As far as possible, this assessment attempts to identify recurrent budget, capital investment budget, and nonbudget amounts.

102. Since 1970, expenditure on education has been reported as consistently high at about 9.4% of gross domestic income (GDI). Figure 5 shows a comparison between Uzbekistan, Azerbaijan, Kazakhstan, the Kyrgyz Republic, Finland, and the Republic of Korea, which suggests that budgets are determined based on a relationship to GDI rather than a demand-side procedure based on the actual system needs. Unlike Uzbekistan, where education expenditure is constant as a proportion of GDI, education spending in other countries fluctuates over time.

103. Table 17 indicates the total recurrent budget shares for the different education subsectors (i.e., excluding centralized investment expenditure). The sparklines for each subsector show that there has been a consistent increase in absolute terms. However, if this is matched against the annual inflation rate over the same period (about 10%), the allocations have remained at about the same level in terms of purchasing parity.

104. Table 18 shows the same data expressed as percentages of the total education expenditure for each year. Here, the sparklines show a very different story, with generally rising percentages for academic lyceum and TVET (and since 2010 for preschool education), and overall decreases in percentages for general secondary and

Figure 5: Comparison of Current Expenditure on Education
(%)

Uzbekistan – Expenditures on Education – Current expenditure on education as a share of gross national income (%)

Current expenditure on education as % GNI is the total public current education expenditure expressed as a percentage of the gross national income (GNI) in a given financial year. GNI is also referred to as gross national product.

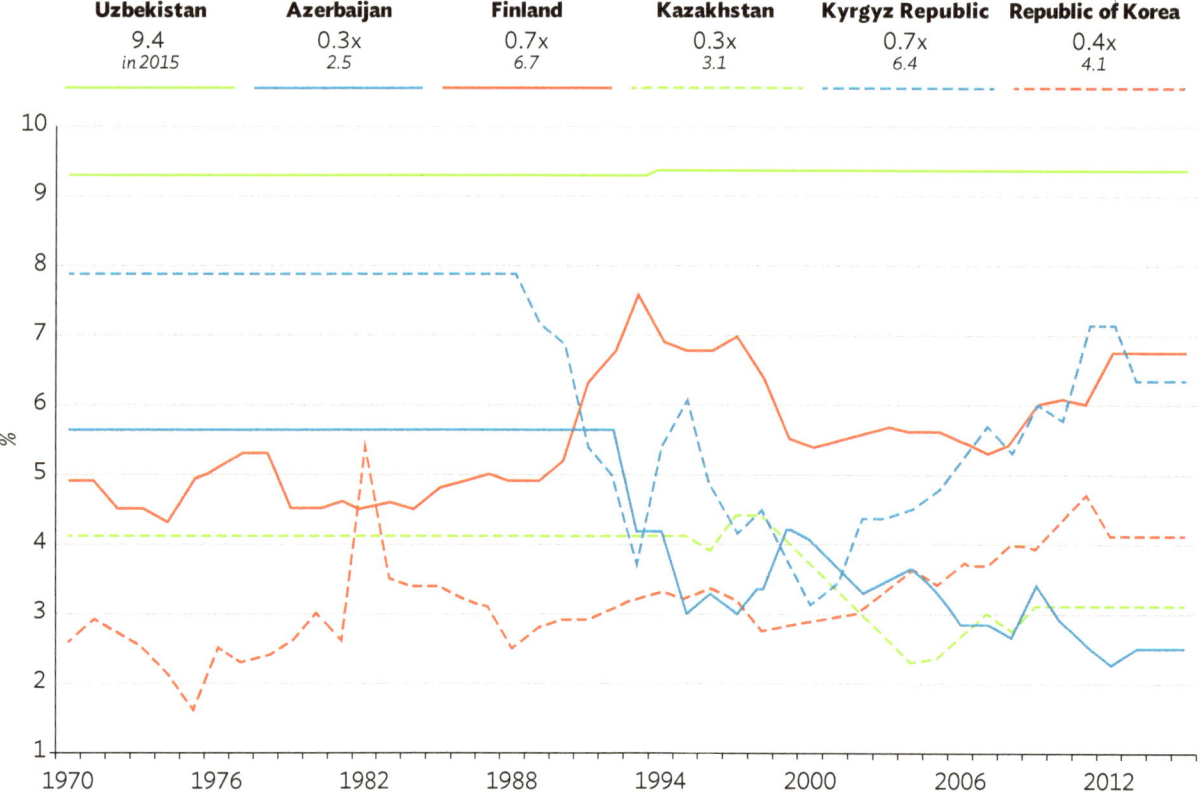

Source: Authors' calculation, based on World Bank data.

higher education. 2016 was the last year of the old 9+3 system (9 years general secondary plus 3 years TVET or academic lyceum), and future trends may greatly differ.

105. TVET colleges are expected to carry out income-generating activities, and recent decrees set the legal basis for this. Resolution 3504 provides a legal basis for funding sources for TVET colleges, based on the principle of self-financing, including funding through the budgets of the new supervising ministries and agencies, funding through the resources of the economic associations, commercial banks and large enterprises, and funding through activities of the colleges themselves (e.g., contract training, consultancy work, publishing).[73]

---

[73] Government of Uzbekistan. 2018. *Resolution of the President. On Improvement of the Activities of the Center of Senior Secondary and Vocational Education under the Ministry of Higher and Secondary Vocational Education of the Republic of Uzbekistan.* No. PP 3504. 3 February.

Table 17: Education Recurrent Budget Expenditure, by Sector, 2005–2016
(SUM billion)

	2005	2006	2007	2008	2009	2010	2011	2012	2013	2014	2015	2016	Sparkline
Preschool education	142.9	170.9	218.7	279.3	361.1	464.3	569.7	738.8	964.8	1,160.0	1,481.6	1,661.4	
General secondary education	633.5	860.9	1,131.6	1,598.9	2,103.2	2,791.4	3,447.8	4,102.9	4,920.7	5,905.6	7,027.0	8,031.9	
Academic lyceums	9.9	14.3	24.5	38.6	57.3	81.3	104.6	128.4	156.2	194.6	235.4	260.7	
Vocational education colleges	124.7	160.0	224.8	365.4	566.0	849.0	1,087.4	1,364.1	1,704.2	2,037.6	2,393.6	2,638.2	
Higher education	59.1	74.5	100.8	149.5	205.7	224.1	302.4	336.7	408.1	483.9	575.2	643.2	
Other personnel training	21.2	20.6	26.5	37.5	39.3	54.0	71.0	56.4	78.3	82.1	109.2	128.7	
Total	991.3	1,301.2	1,726.9	2,469.2	3,332.6	4,464.1	5,582.9	6,727.3	8,232.3	9,863.8	11,822.0	13,364.1	

Source: United Nations Children's Fund.

Table 18: Education Recurrent Budget Expenditure, by Sector
(%)

	2005	2006	2007	2008	2009	2010	2011	2012	2013	2014	2015	2016	Sparkline
Preschool education	14.4	13.1	12.7	11.3	10.8	10.4	10.2	11.0	11.7	11.8	12.5	12.4	
General secondary education	78.3	79.3	78.3	76.0	73.9	73.0	71.9	72.0	71.4	71.6	72.0	72.5	
Academic lyceums	1.0	1.1	1.4	1.6	1.7	1.8	1.9	1.9	1.9	2.0	2.0	2.0	
Vocational education colleges	12.6	12.3	13.0	14.8	17.0	19.0	19.5	20.3	20.7	20.7	20.2	19.7	
Higher education	6.0	5.7	5.8	6.1	6.2	5.0	5.4	5.0	5.0	4.9	4.9	4.8	
Other personnel training	2.1	1.6	1.5	1.5	1.2	1.2	1.3	0.8	1.0	0.8	0.9	1.0	
Total	100.0	100.0	100.0	100.0	100.0	100.0	100.0	100.0	100.0	100.0	100.0	100.0	

Source: United Nations Children's Fund.

ii. Public Expenditures and Application of Generated Funds

106. Education expenditure as a percentage of gross national income (for three subsectors: general secondary, TVET, and higher education) dropped slightly until 2017 (actuals), with a slight rise in 2018 (budgeted) (Figure 6). However, the figures for 2017 and 2018 are affected by the reform of post-grade-9 education and the subsequent reductions in enrollments in TVET and academic lyceums, so any trends must be treated with caution.

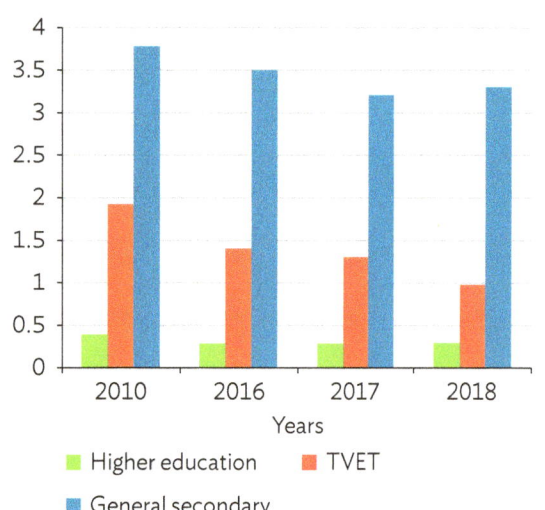

Figure 6: Government Expenditure on Three Education Subsectors as a Percentage of Gross Domestic Product (%)

TVET = technical and vocational education and training.
Notes: (i) Timeline is not to scale.
(ii) 2010 to 2017 figures are actuals; 2018 figures are estimates.
Source: Ministry of Finance.

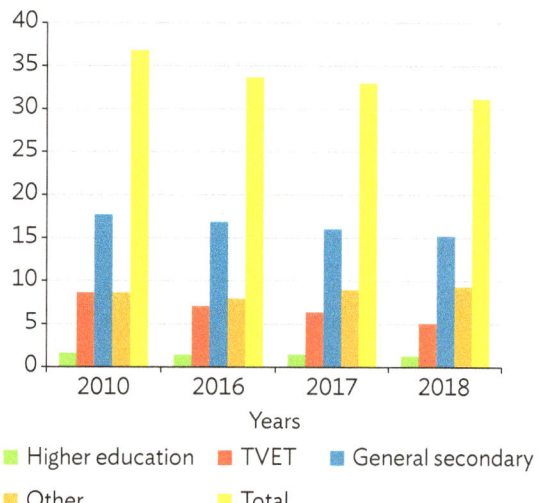

Figure 7: Government Expenditure on Education Subsectors as a Percentage of Government Expenditure

TVET = technical and vocational education and training.
Notes: (i) Timeline is not to scale.
(ii) 2010 to 2017 figures are actuals; 2018 figures are estimates.
Source: Ministry of Finance.

107. It is clear, however, that government expenditure on education is being maintained at its current high level (over 30% of total government expenditure) as shown in Figure 7.

108. Table 19 is a breakdown of the total on-budget and off-budget expenditure on education. Recurrent spending covers all education costs including in-service training of education personnel (about 27% of the total on-budget amount until 2011, after which the two lines were combined). In 2016, actual on-budget recurrent expenditure amounted to about 91% of total government spending on education.

109. Income generation by institutions is encouraged, and funds generated are retained 100% by the institutions for use as a "college fund." Before 2018, up to 25% of the funds could be used as salary supplements or overtime, and 75% for purchase of materials, or other general use (footnote 53). This retention of funds by the colleges continues under the new arrangements and is indeed encouraged as part of the overall funding of college operations. It is not currently clear whether the old 25%:75% split will be applied. Special consideration is given to free education for students from low-income families, as well as confirming the requirement that graduates who were state-funded will be required to work for 3 years in the regions on completion of their courses. A new TVET college admissions policy is also to be established.

iii. Private Spending

110. Until the proposed household surveys have been completed, it is not possible to estimate with any degree of accuracy the contributions made by students and parents to the funding of the TVET sector.[74] TVET students will need to pay fees for tuition and also bear the costs of uniforms, although students from poor households are

---

[74] In the case of higher education, student contracts (fees and costs paid by students) account for about 65% of total expenditures.

Table 19: Total Budgetary and Nonbudgetary Expenditure on Education
(SUM billion)

	2012	2013	2014	2015	2016
Overall expenditures including personnel training (Total on-budget funds)	**6,727.1**	**8,232.3**	**9,863.7**	**11,822.0**	**13,364.2**
Expenditures on financing centralized investments into education	*Included in fund for reconstruction, renovating, and equipping educational and medical institutions (below)*				
Fund for reconstruction, renovating, and equipping educational and medical institutions	691.0	807.1	998.1	1,151.5	1,229.7
Fund for development of children's sports	5.2	8.3	10.1	12.2	15.4
Total Nonbudgetary Funds	696.2	815.4	1,008.2	1,163.7	1,245.1
Grand Total	7,423.3	9,047.7	10,871.9	12,985.7	14,609.3

Source: United Nations Children's Fund.

exempted. Learning materials are generally made available through the college library, and college funds are used to purchase consumables for practical training. TVET will be provided free of charge to students in professional schools (along with three meals per day), but other TVET institutes will charge tuition fees. Opportunity costs of TVET have not previously been an issue as TVET was part of the 12-year (9+3) compulsory education. However, with the onset of elective TVET, opportunity costs will become a factor in decisions related to continuing professional education and training.

iv. Unit Costs

111. Generally, recurrent budget expenditure is split between teacher salaries (90%) and teaching and learning resources (10%). A simple calculation of total recurrent expenditure divided by total enrollment by sector gives an indicative "per capita" amount spent per subsector in absolute terms (Figure 8). Per capita spending per subsector shows a steady increase spread almost equally between the subsectors (x-axis shows Uzbek sum), though with a slightly higher rate of increase for academic lyceums. If this figure is compared with Figure 4 (trends in post-secondary enrollments), the apparent increase in per capita spending (121.4%) is explained by the decline in enrollments (13.7%), indicating that budgeting for the sector is based on factors other than student numbers. A similar situation applies to academic lyceums (enrollments declined by 9.5% while "per capita" expenditure increased by 124.5%). During the same period, higher education enrollments increased by 3.9% while "per capita" expenditure increased by 83.9%, and general secondary (including all formal grades 1–9 pupils) enrollments increased by 7.4%, while "per capita" expenditure increased by 81.3%.

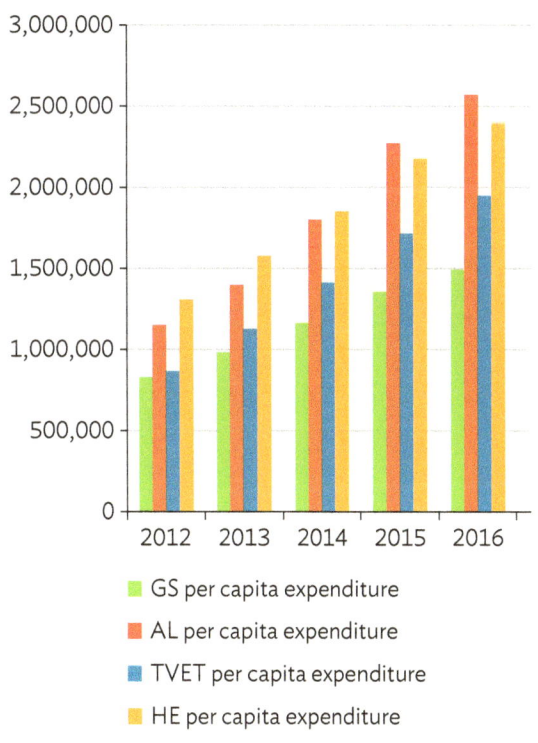

Figure 8: Simple Calculation of per Capita Expenditure by Sector, 2012–2016
(SUM)

AL = academic lyceum, GS = general secondary, HE = higher education, TVET = technical and vocational education and training.
Sources: Authors' calculations based on data from State Statistics Committee and United Nations Children's Fund.

III. Challenges and Opportunities

A. Demand for Technical and Vocational Education and Training Programs

112. As noted above, it is difficult to forecast TVET enrollments with any degree of reliability beyond the estimate of about 0.8 million students in AY2019/2020. In any case, student demand for TVET programs will decline rapidly in the immediate future, with many colleges destined to be closed as a result of government reforms. However, the reduction in current demand provides a window of opportunity in relation to some of the other reforms. The new policies place great emphasis on making TVET programs more competency-based, with focus on a better balance between theory and practical work, greater focus on skills development (nontechnical skills as well as technical), entrepreneurship as a cross-cutting domain, and better-monitored work practice and internships, thus changing the entire TVET sector into a learner-oriented and competency-based delivery system. This places huge demands on the teaching staff of the colleges, who will need to be supported with professional development programs, training, and/or retraining in competency-based methodologies. The old division between teachers (for theoretical work) and masters (for practical work) will become less clear as theory and practice become better integrated. The lower demand for TVET during the next few years will mean a reduction in teaching loads for many, if not all, staff. This will, therefore, provide a good opportunity to organize the needed training and continuous professional development programs.

113. The move to demand-driven education has so far only considered demand from education consumers—the students (and their parents). Demand for skilled and qualified personnel from the employers' perspective has not been thoroughly considered. Thus, it is not known whether employers will recognize the new qualifications as meeting their needs for skilled workers or whether they will expect "junior diploma" holders to complete TVET programs at the colleges before employing them.

114. Several conditions must be satisfied before reliable estimates of student demand for TVET programs can be made: the new general education curricula must be in place and the anticipated types and levels of skills and knowledge must be made known to the employers; employers' opinions regarding the suitability and relevance of the new qualifications must be surveyed; a robust careers guidance model must be established to ensure pupils are aware of the limitations of the "junior" qualifications and the benefits of pursuing further education in TVET college or elsewhere. The theoretical capacity of the 1,046 TVET colleges that will remain in operation after the reform is fully implemented is about 1 million students, but this number may be reduced by the need to accommodate a school production and training units (UPKs) in each TVET college.[75] In Table 9, a purely arbitrary figure of 50% of graduates has been used to estimate immediate demand for places in TVET. Similarly, potential academic lyceum admissions could be at about 50% to match the roughly 50% reduction in the number of academic lyceums.

---

[75] The UPK strategy has been discontinued by the government. De facto UPKs functioned in some schools only in AY2018/2019. The Ministry of Public Education plans to introduce a career guidance system from grade 7 and expand the number of elective courses in grades 8 and 9 (see https://www.gazeta.uz/ru/2020/07/14/professional-education/).

B. Linking Demand for Technical and Vocational Education and Training with Demand for Skills

115. In terms of student selection of their field of study, the linking of TVET program intake quotas to student demand, as defined by the regional development plans, is clearly becoming more sophisticated, and micro and small enterprises (MSEs) can make increasing contributions to the process. The establishment of sector skills councils[76] and other nationwide and profession-wide mechanisms are still a long way off (except in the tourism sector). Nevertheless, increased participation on a local level is a good start, both feeding into the skills demand and development processes and providing opportunities for networking and collaboration between entrepreneurs from different business sectors. The latter is internationally seen as crucial to the success of small and medium-sized businesses.

116. Observed declines in enrollment in computer science and communication technologies are puzzling (Table 10). Further information and analysis on employers' skills requirements and on trends in employment opportunities are needed to answer such questions. The enrollment trends in the health sector are also declining, but the health sector programs have consistently been oversubscribed—many more health workers are trained than are needed by the employment market. This situation does not seem to reconcile with the current setting of training quotas according to regional development plans.

117. In summary, there are mechanisms in place for determining how many and what types of graduates will be needed in each region over the short term, and employers contribute to the process. However, there seem to be exceptions to this rule, leading to overproduction of graduates in certain professions such as health. Thus, the current system for creating employable entrants to the labor market appears to be relatively robust and is well-established. However, it is a system developed mainly to provide workers in large-scale enterprises, which are designed to meet domestic demand. The formal TVET system is closely linked with the enterprises in question, which are a source of both physical and informational resources, receiving in return a steady supply of new employees. This is clearly a strength of the system and should be built upon, but it must also be recognized that the system does not promote worker mobility or adaptability, either laterally (in terms of changing employer—especially between regions or occupation) or vertically (in terms of career or wage progression).

118. The system does not meet the needs of MSEs. The current TVET system produces graduates with narrow skill sets based on traditional occupational skills (toolmaking, welding, bookkeeping, cooking, auto-mechanics, and others). MSEs need to be able to find people with several different kinds of skill sets. Graduates receiving support for start-ups through the government policy of promoting entrepreneurship will need to have both the technical and soft skills related to their chosen profession such as marketing, IT, management, communication, and other skills. Indeed, as the large enterprises begin to look more toward export markets, they will also need workers with different combinations of skill sets.

C. Learning Outputs: Quality

119. This section analyzes the challenges to quality of the delivered TVET in Uzbekistan by considering the overall delivery process from identification of the need for TVET graduates to the monitoring of the TVET system via tracer studies, and others. In section E, this analysis is used to identify how business sector involvement can contribute to improvement and further development of the TVET system.

---

[76] Sector skills councils are a mechanism for developing dynamic and demand-based TVET planning. They help to establish a common understanding of the skills required for specific occupations to meet the requirements of the labor market through links between TVET providers and industry.

i. Careers Education and Guidance

120. Careers education and guidance (CEG) is identified as one of the weak links of the TVET system, resulting in students dropping out of programs. Students mostly choose TVET education based on their parents' opinion and on expected future monetary income. This leads to low interest among students, which further leads to low skills levels. Current data do not permit accurate assessment of dropout rates, but the authors' calculations from data available (see Table 7) shows 96.7% of the 2011 TVET intake and 97.2% of the 2012 intake graduated after 3 years of study, indicating dropout and/or failure rates of about 3%. However, in 2016, 102% of the 2013 intake graduated, indicating some degree of repetition of years. This view was supported by a response that some students drop out, but are encouraged to return later to pick up their studies again. It is not currently known how prevalent this is.

121. During the first year of TVET, students take only general subjects and make visits to companies to look at their chosen professional field in practice. If students have not visited companies prior to these visits (during the general secondary education) it is already late because their career selection has already been made and the TVET program has already begun. As a part of the enrollment process, TVET college representatives visit the public schools when the number of needed students is known. During this visit, the college would inform the students about the vacant positions. This is a narrow view of career guidance and in reality is simply information provision. Once the TVET college students graduate it is common to use job fairs as a way to match companies and students (the employer survey showed 32% of the respondents expressing interest in participation in job fairs).[77] The survey asked employers how they would like to help improve the current TVET system. The answers were very positive for activities that can potentially be used to improve CEG, so there is strong interest from the employers to engage in activities directly linked to CEG:

(i) 65% of employers are willing to organize shorter company visits for groups of students;
(ii) 39% of employers are willing to participate in job fairs; and
(iii) 29% of employers are willing to give guest lectures at the local TVET institution.

122. Overall, CEG needs to be improved to ensure that students are choosing training and education that are in accordance with what they are able and willing to engage in and what possible opportunities are in line. This will ensure that they enjoy their time in college, become competent, and later engage in lifelong learning. The positive side is that companies are interested in engaging with the institutions in improving CEG.

ii. Curriculum

123. The TVET curriculum is theoretically based on occupational competency standards, but in fact, it is based on the classification for each occupation, which sets out the needed knowledge levels, but not the skills required.

124. **The employer survey reveals how employers assess the training content provided by TVET institutes.** A little over 30% of respondents answered that graduates are employed below the level of qualification because they do not have enough skills, and 10% replied that graduates do not have the right type of skills. In addition, only 50% of respondents replied that knowledge and skills of TVET graduates are relevant to the job. These responses indicate that the curriculum is not in line with labor market demand as seen from the employers' point of view. Employers' suggestions for improving the TVET curriculum are in Table 20.

125. The survey explored the potential content of a new curriculum. Employers were asked to indicate the importance of a set of personal characteristics, basic skills, and job-related skills that they look for in new employees. These are skills employers would like TVET colleges to focus on to provide a more relevant labor force—technical skills, cooperative skills, personal skills, thinking skills and innovation, and business skills. Some of the results are presented in Figure 9.

---

[77] ADB. Forthcoming. *Skills Needs Assessment for Micro and Small Enterprises in Uzbekistan: Enterprise Survey Report* (footnote 2).

Table 20: Employers' Suggestions for Improvements to the Technical and Vocational Education and Training Curriculum

Responses	No. of Respondents
Related to practice versus theory	**52**
Increase practice	44
Conduct practice in a real place	1
Practice should be strengthened by monitoring	3
Other	4
Content of education	**25**
Deep study of modern technology	9
Pay attention to culture	5
Better computer skills	4
Ethics	3
Other	4
Training should focus on specialty	**22**
Training with specialist	16
Technical subjects	2
Graduates lack even simple technical skills and others	3

Source: ADB. 2022. *Skills Needs Assessment for Micro and Small Enterprises in Uzbekistan: Enterprise Survey Report*. Manila: Prepared for ADB. Uzbekistan: Skills Strategies for Industrial Modernization and Inclusive Growth. Manila (TA 9256-UZB).

Figure 9: Skills Required by Employers
(%)

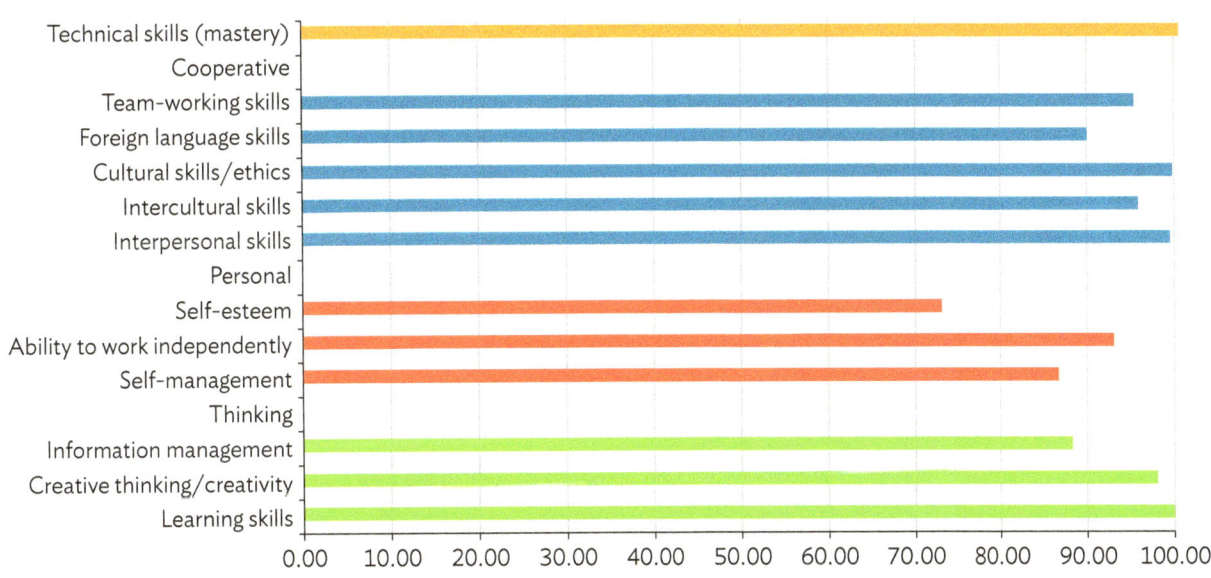

Source: ADB. 2022. *Skills Needs Assessment for Micro and Small Enterprises in Uzbekistan: Enterprise Survey Report*. Manila: Prepared for ADB. Uzbekistan: Skills Strategies for Industrial Modernization and Inclusive Growth. Manila (TA 9256-UZB).

126.   Technical skills and learning skills were accorded the highest priority. Cultural or ethics and interpersonal skills were considered next in importance.

127.   To further deepen the analysis of employers' requirements, employers were asked what qualities are most looked for during recruitment; the level of education/training was highest or second priority for 80% of employers, followed by good person-to-person skills (i.e., communication, teamworking, and others).

128.   Thus, technical competencies are ranked highest, followed by soft skills developed through interactive teaching methods. These responses also match well with the overall picture that TVET graduates do not have all the technical competencies in demand in the labor market. The responses also highlight the importance of developing soft skills during education and training, either as key modules and/or as cross-cutting training activities.

iii.   Teaching Staff

129.   Generally, teachers and masters are not connected with businesses and, thus, tend to lack experience of "real-job" situations and practices. Professional development of teaching staff is, thus, a crucial area that needs to be strengthened. Teachers need to be connected with companies; currently, too many teachers come directly from universities and lack practical experience. Teachers often lack the professional capacity to train students in the use of specific equipment. In contrast, at the Korea International Cooperation Agency (KOICA) PTC, many of the teachers come with an industry background and some have previously been working as teachers in the initial vocational education and training (iVET) system. Many of these teachers have been trained in the Republic of Korea.

130.   There are clear differences in capabilities between colleges. The director of one of Uzbekistan's top TVET colleges mentioned the teachers and masters as the main reason for their success; students interviewed at the college all mentioned that the teachers are very good, supporting their progress including preparing business plans. However, the general professional level of TVET teachers is expressed as a weakness of the TVET system. Improving continuous professional development for teachers and masters should be a priority, and entrepreneurs have expressed their support for this process. About 20% of survey respondents mentioned issues related to education content and teachers in relation to the information they want to get from the local TVET colleges.

131.   One of the problematic issues is that salaries are usually higher in the private sector than in the public sector, so it is often difficult to attract teachers and masters from the private sector. In the survey, employers were not directly asked about the quality of teachers and masters, but were asked for suggestions as to how the VET system could be improved: 15% of respondents mentioned teachers and teaching as a focus for improvement (Table 21).

132.   The survey asked what kind of information employers would like to receive from the TVET system: 15% supported a stronger cooperation between educational institutions and employers, including aspects related to teaching staff, and a further 18% detailed the forms of public–private cooperation they support (Table 22).

iv.   Implementation

133.   There is a high level of local support for the implementation of TVET, though there appear to be wide differences across colleges. In particular, the entrepreneurial courses were well regarded, and many students presented new ideas for start-ups. In the banking college, the entrepreneurial course was 40 hours: with 22 hours theory and 18 hours practical. It included three areas: (i) business planning, (ii) obtaining credit, and (iii) finding a job.

Table 21: Employers' Suggestions for How to Improve the Quality of Teaching

Teachers and Teaching	No. of Respondents
Improve the quality of teaching	8
Improve teachers' own knowledge, including practical knowledge	3
Increase number of qualified teachers	4
Technical specialist should have minimum 1 year of practice as in the medical field	1
Appoint qualified teachers as tutors	1
Strengthen professional development of teachers	1
Provide modern training tools	1
Total	**19**

Source: ADB. 2022. *Skills Needs Assessment for Micro and Small Enterprises in Uzbekistan: Enterprise Survey Report.* Manila: Prepared for ADB. Uzbekistan: Skills Strategies for Industrial Modernization and Inclusive Growth. Manila (TA 9256-UZB).

Table 22: Employers' Suggestions for How to Improve Cooperation

Responses	Number of Respondents
Cooperation between business and educational institutions	**17**
Colleges together with employers should introduce new students to the production processes	5
Companies should go to educational institutions and observe the educational process	3
Companies can take interns	3
Students should have the opportunity to visit companies at least once to be acquainted with work processes	2
Colleges should share knowledge with experienced specialists	2
Entrepreneurs, teachers, and alumni should meet and discuss	1
Cooperation between schools and companies	**15**
Offers of internships and summer practice	12
Colleges, businesses, and parents should work together	2
Employers should give lectures at colleges	2
Cooperation on educational content and teacher development	15
Employers should assist in raising professional level of the teacher, methods of training, and quality of education	10
Employers should assist in development of new curricula	3
Employers should assist in raising the practical and technical skills of college staff	2

Source: ADB. 2022. *Skills Needs Assessment for Micro and Small Enterprises in Uzbekistan: Enterprise Survey Report.* Manila: Prepared for ADB. Uzbekistan: Skills Strategies for Industrial Modernization and Inclusive Growth. Manila (TA 9256-UZB).

134. On the other hand, it was mentioned many times, that "theory is in the TVET college and practice is in the companies." A weakness of the TVET system identified by entrepreneurs was that "receiving knowledge does not equal knowing." In a general analysis of the strengths, weaknesses, opportunities, and threats (SWOT) in the Andijan region, "language skills," "technical skills," and "education system" were mentioned as weaknesses. There were similar mentions of mismatch in the level of language needed in companies and what the graduates have. On the other hand, "foreign language" was mentioned as a strength of the Navoi region. Many students at two TVET colleges in Andijan spoke English very well, having the skills to present their business plans. However, many of them mentioned that they took extra classes after school.

135. The compulsory internships (during the 3-year programs) were described as working well by both students and companies. Students in a cooking class explained that internships provide an opportunity to try out in practice what they learn in the college. The director of a company that takes a lot of TVET students for internships in Andijan explained that internship was satisfactory. He also noted that in the beginning, they give students simple tasks to slowly develop their competence. Several of the companies mentioned that when they have third year internships, they assess the students and usually they sign a contract with the students who are qualified. Hence, the internship also works as a tool to ensure smooth and fast entry into the labor market.

136. In contrast, lack of supervision in internships is identified by colleges themselves as a weakness of the TVET system. This included the students' work environment as well. In contrast, the professional training centers established with KOICA support provide 4 months of the 10-month courses as internships.

137. It is evident that the main problem in implementation is the lack of practice. Most education and training is provided by teachers and/or masters with higher education. The facilities might be reasonable, but when equipment is outdated and little or no materials and supplies are available, it is impossible to implement practical work. There is currently no mechanism in place that would allow employers to contribute regularly to decisions on the provision of equipment or new workshop or laboratory requirements for TVET colleges. Equipment and facilities are mainly designed to serve generic training needs.

v. Assessment

138. Employers repeatedly mentioned that the assessment of the internship periods could be improved. The overall impression is that assessment is based on the old style, with assessment of each student being noted in the journal and a written test used to assess knowledge learned. The concepts of competency-based assessment, as well as formative and summative assessment, have been discussed with stakeholders; it was clear that the terms formative and summative were neither used nor implemented. Similarly, the National Testing Center only prepares and implements written tests.

139. Teachers will need special training to carry out competency-based assessment, because they do not have enough experience in different types of assessment.

vi. Graduate Outcomes

140. The TVET system is not generally seen as a route to higher education, with only 3% continuing to higher education. Alarmingly, only 40% of graduates who find a job are employed in their area of specialization. This is either because there are no employment opportunities in that area, indicating that TVET institutes educate students in areas that are not in demand, or it is because the graduates do not have the competencies needed to be employed as a specialist.

141. The above findings from the survey are in line with previous studies. A World Bank report from 2014, which was based on an in-depth survey of over 200 enterprises in Uzbekistan, documented that only 57% of surveyed firms were satisfied with the skills of TVET graduates, versus 79% for university graduates.[78] A United Nations Development Programme (UNDP) report from 2008 found that only 61% of graduates from professional colleges were in employment after graduation and only 45% of graduates found a job in a field that corresponds to their vocation.[79]

---

[78] World Bank. 2014. *Uzbekistan Modernizing Tertiary Education*. Washington, DC.
[79] UNDP. 2008. *Education in Uzbekistan: Matching Supply and Demand. National Human Development Report (2007/08)*. Tashkent.

142. On the positive side, the number of graduates engaged in entrepreneurial activities seems promising. Commercial banks allocated SUM54 billion in soft loans to graduated students based on business plans developed pregraduation. If the number of entrepreneurs is proportionally the same for the 46% of graduates for which there is no information, about 4% of graduates engage in entrepreneurial activities immediately after graduation.

143. This aspect was also confirmed during visits to TVET colleges. Many students had plans for starting their own business. The director of one college explained that in the previous year, 10 students took credit to start a business and that on average about 10%–15% of graduates start their own business. About 10% of graduates from this same college go on to higher education—more than three times the national average.

144. Almost 50% of graduates were recruited through graduates contacting the employer directly. About 10% were recruited by "student agency in an education institute," and only about 20% through the public employment services (PES) (Figure 10).

145. An identified weakness of the TVET system is that graduates are not fully employable and need retraining before they become employable. This view is confirmed by the results of the ADB employer survey. Respondents were asked to assess the relevance to the labor market of the education and training provided by higher education, academic lyceums, and TVET colleges. Only 21% of respondents replied that the education and training provided by TVET colleges was *relevant*, and 32% said it was *not relevant*. The remainder responded that it was *partly relevant*. This clearly indicates that the TVET system is not adequately in line with labor market demand. Almost 60% of employers were of the opinion that knowledge and skills of TVET graduates met their

Figure 10: Employer Responses on Their Use of Different Recruitment Processes
(%)

Source: ADB. 2022. *Skills Needs Assessment for Micro and Small Enterprises in Uzbekistan: Enterprise Survey Report.* Manila: Prepared for ADB. Uzbekistan: Skills Strategies for Industrial Modernization and Inclusive Growth. Manila (TA 9256-UZB).

expectations. Taken together with the 21% of employers who think TVET training is relevant, this may be an indication that most employers have a low expectation of the TVET system.

146. Graduates of TVET colleges are mostly employed in production (39% of males and 47% of females). Employers were asked to consider the TVET college graduates recruited since 2014. The answers confirm that many of these graduates are not employed in positions related to their qualification. Almost 60% of males and only 40% of females are employed in a position related to the field of competencies of the qualification. In addition, almost 40% of males and females are not employed at the level of their qualification; about 60% of employers employ TVET college graduates below the level of their qualification. More than 30% of employers stated that graduates do not have enough skills, and more than 10% stated that the graduates do not have the right type of skills.

147. Conversely, employers were also asked why they employ someone above the level of their qualification. It seems that experience has the biggest influence. This is confirmed by the more than 20% who answer that the person has other important skills that are not part of the qualification. These skills will most likely come from experience, e.g., in a managerial or similar supervisory role. This indicates that important working skills are not currently being taught in TVET institutes.

vii. Quality Assurance

148. There is no systematic and comprehensive quality assurance (QA) process in the current TVET system, though, MHSSE has planned to set up such a system. However, it is unclear how this will be implemented. Decree 5313 sets out some guidelines for the proposed QA system.[80] Item 2 in the decree sets out the most important tasks of the system of professional training in vocational education. These are focused on a closer cooperation between the TVET system and the labor market, as well as mentioning international qualification frameworks. All these tasks can potentially be used in definition of quality indicators and mechanisms for an effective QA system. Overall, the decree gives a clear indication that the changes in the TVET system also include a more comprehensive approach to QA.

viii. Institutional Management

149. The management functions of TVET colleges are generally centered around the director, and most of the work done by the board of trustees is focused on internal affairs. The management group of a TVET college, therefore, includes the director, deputy directors, and the pedagogical council. Stakeholders in each TVET college are students, employers (state-owned industries, private companies), parents, government (economy, budget), society (labor market, export), funding agencies, teachers, and the *khokimyat*. TVET college boards of trustees are more akin to advisory boards as they lack an oversight role, but rather provide strategic advice to the management of TVET colleges.

D. Continuing Vocational Education and Training

150. There is no systematic offering of CVET courses in existing TVET institutes. Some courses are offered for retraining of unemployed job seekers, such as those organized by KOICA-financed PTCs. However, the survey shows high demand for CVET. More than half of female TVET graduates and almost 20% of male graduates participated in organized training offered by their employers. About 50% of training was done via mentoring by senior staff within the company, and about 25% of training was in-house (side-by-side) training. Overall, about 75% of training was done within the company (Figure 11). This indicates that companies are experienced in delivering training, and they have staff who have been engaged in training activities as mentor and/or trainer.

---

[80] Government of Uzbekistan. 2018. Decree of the President (footnote 25).

151. In addition, about 40% of female graduates and almost 20% of male graduates participated in external training in a work-related field. However, 55% of the employers interviewed responded that training is available, but not relevant. This reinforces the view that the skills being imparted by TVET training institutes are not in line with labor market demands.

Figure 11: **Types of Training Delivery Considered in the Employer Survey**

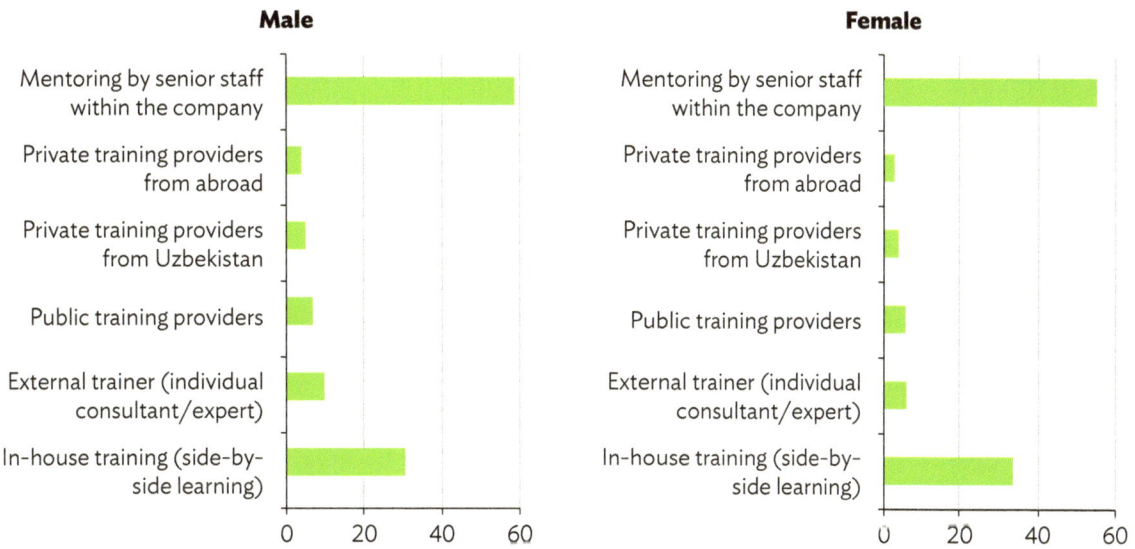

Source: ADB. 2022. *Skills Needs Assessment for Micro and Small Enterprises in Uzbekistan: Enterprise Survey Report.* Manila: Prepared for ADB. Uzbekistan: Skills Strategies for Industrial Modernization and Inclusive Growth. Manila (TA 9256-UZB).

IV. Labor Market Outcomes

A. Labor Market: An Aggregate Picture

152. With global competition increasing, demographic change unfolding, and rapid technological change intensifying, skills mismatch has entered the policy debate on a global scale. Skills mismatch refers not only to skill shortages or gaps, but also to situations where qualifications, knowledge, and skills exceed job requirements. Shortages in some sectors may occur simultaneously with gluts in others. When skills mismatch takes time to resolve, it imposes real costs on individuals, enterprises, and training institutes. In Uzbekistan, substantial changes are challenging the labor market and contributing to jobs mismatch and skills shortages. Large numbers of employers complain that they cannot find workers with the skills their businesses require. At the same time, many TVET graduates have difficulty finding jobs that match their qualifications.

153. People entering the labor market face problems in finding jobs matching their skills and potential. At the same time, structural trends challenge the economy of the country to provide the skills that economies need to grow and prosper. The dynamics of today's labor markets not only create new jobs while others shrink or disappear, but also contribute to changing skill requirements in many existing jobs.

154. Uzbekistan is undergoing significant reforms as the economy is opening, both domestically and internationally. Decentralization, privatization of state-owned enterprises, and PPPs are only part of the reform program underway in Uzbekistan. The ongoing reforms adopt varied approaches: improving the efficiency of existing, and creating new, free economic zones, technoparks, small industrial zones; expansion of lending to promising investment projects, as well as small and medium-sized enterprises; creation of jobs and ensuring rational employment, especially for graduates of secondary and higher education institutions, and ensuring the balance and development of labor market infrastructure; reducing unemployment; improving the training and employment of students of TVET in skills areas that meet the requirements of the market economy and the needs of employers; improving the quality and effectiveness of higher education institutions through introduction of international standards of training and assessment of the quality of teaching; gradual increase in admission quota in higher education institutions; employment and engaging in private entrepreneurship of graduates of secondary specialized, vocational, and higher education institutions.

155. The recognition of skills mismatch as a key challenge and the lack of information on the labor force requirements of micro and small enterprises (MSEs) have increased the imperative to develop methods to monitor, analyze, and anticipate skills mismatch as crucial tools for the planning of educational provision. Monitoring and assessing mismatch and its effects involves much more than straightforward comparisons between skill needs and skill supply. Skills mismatch is a complex phenomenon, affecting individuals, enterprises, training providers, economies, and societies.

156. Uzbekistan lacks reliable information available to assist youth and adults in making career decisions. Available information provided by the National Scientific Center for Employment and Labor Protection or State Statistics Committee is available only as raw data and there is little analysis carried out on these data. On the one hand, further development of career guidance and career planning services are obviously needed. This entails a better labor market information system that involves the timely collection and analysis of labor market trends, and the training of specialists to use this information to effectively advise graduates, job seekers, and employers. On the other hand, there is a need to monitor the evolution of labor market trends, including new jobs and skills in demand to adapt measures to the changes, and to regularly update the information that could be provided to the beneficiaries mentioned above.

157. As part of the country's continuing efforts to take advantage of its young and growing population and make better use of its human capital, policy makers in Uzbekistan are working to understand the individual skills needed to bring about better labor market outcomes. Further, policy makers aim to design policies and programs to improve the skills of labor market participants. The recent draft project on lifelong learning in 2018–2025 is one example of this approach.[81]

B. The Demand Side

158. During the last decades, sweeping changes have occurred as the country has been moving from a state-planned economy to a demand-driven market economy. While the influence of large state companies is decreasing, MSEs have been creating jobs. From the labor market perspective, MSEs are the sector driving employment opportunities and making major contributions to the economy—their main objective is a quick search for and recruitment of highly skilled personnel, capable of adding immediate value to the company.

159. The biggest challenge is linked with selection and recruitment of qualified technical staff in a situation where there is a shortage of qualified youth with work experience and who also understand career opportunities. Often, young people enter the labor market with high salary expectations, only to be disappointed and demotivated when confronted with the realities of employment.

160. The lack of fully qualified technical staff in the labor market is compensated by qualified, or sometimes underqualified, but experienced, older personnel. However, here too, many experienced professionals are striving to find opportunities for contractual employment and projects abroad, which offer higher salaries. This also contributes to the lack of qualified technical staff in the country. In short, there is strong and growing demand in the labor market for appropriate technical skills and work experience. The role of the TVET system must, therefore, be to provide, with as little delay as possible, its graduates with at least the needed skill sets and a better understanding of the responsibilities of employment, careers pathways, and a realistic view of salaries and benefits that can accrue from working.

161. An additional demand-side issue relates to the recognition of Uzbek qualifications outside the country, as well as recognition of lifelong learning and work-based learning (WBL), both within and outside the country. There is an urgent need to establish assessment processes and opportunities for individuals to receive better recognized certification of their actual competencies.

---

[81] Institute for Social Research at the Cabinet of Ministers. 2018. National Strategy of the Republic of Uzbekistan in Educational Sphere of Lifelong Learning for the Period 2018–2025 (Draft). Tashkent.

C. The Supply Side

162. There is a need to secure annually the employment of about 500,000 graduates from specialized secondary, vocational, and higher education institutions. According to the World Bank, the labor force in Uzbekistan was 15.3 million in 2017, while the number of employed was 13.5 million and the number of unemployed was 837,000. The unemployment rate stood at 5.2% in 2018.

163. Table 23 indicates the employment rate of TVET college graduates. It shows that, on average, the employment rate of TVET college graduates was 43% during 2011–2016. The rate shows an increasing trend since 2013, with a slight dip to 53.8% of graduates employed in 2016. This compares with the average 91.4% of students who were able to enter into an agreement on internship during the same period.

Table 23: Employment and Internship Data for Technical and Vocational Education and Training College Graduates, 2011–2016

Indicator	2011	2012	2013	2014	2015	2016	Total
Number of graduates from TVET colleges ('000)	430.2	501.5	501.4	495.2	482.6	456.8	2,888.7
Number of graduates who found employment ('000)	176.2	204.2	181.5	186.6	252.8	245.9	1,238.2
Employment rate (%)	43.7	44.6	41.3	41.8	55.8	53.8	42.9
Number of graduates with tripartite internship contracts ('000)	403.0	457.4	439.2	446.0	453.2	442.6	2,641.4
Percentage of students who had internship in a company (%)	93.7	91.2	87.6	90.1	93.9	92.6	91.4

TVET = technical and vocational education and training.
Source: Ministry of Higher and Secondary Specialized Education.

D. Matching Supply and Demand

164. Access to jobs in Uzbekistan is still influenced by the systems that existed during the period of the former Soviet Union, when the TVET system was focused on training students in skills for positions in state companies. Such enterprises were able to absorb all graduates entering the labor market. There was no real job description with a full list of needed skills, as it seems that, for instance, it was very easy to get the diploma as a welder and to adapt immediately to the work of a welder in a state company. This situation has changed significantly, and the decreasing state sector is not able to absorb the 500,000 entrants into the labor market every year. It means new graduates must use other means of finding jobs: acquiring additional knowledge and skills to increase their employability; learning job techniques on how to find a job (e.g., writing CVs, interview techniques, job information seeking); receiving adequate labor market information; participating in job fairs; contacting employers; registering in PES; or being self employed by creating their own business. Unfortunately, available information is scant; labor market information is weak.

165. Improvements in matching supply and demand could be linked with the establishment of new structures, as well as active measures implemented by the government. At a minimum, several improvements could be contemplated:

(i) A better approach to labor market monitoring, including regional observatories responsible for conducting surveys of employers from representative economic sectors in the region to get an overview of the trends in those sectors, reliable information about jobs and skills in demand, and related staff training needs, while strengthening the links with the employers from the private sector. Better labor market information could facilitate graduates' integration into the labor market, including through strengthening networking among sector stakeholders.

(ii) A framework at the national level that sets out overarching laws and rules, supported by systems at the regional or local level to match skills demand and supply. State funds could be allocated to regions to develop active labor market policies (ALMPs) with stakeholders playing a role in labor market monitoring and developing public–private partnerships.

(iii) ALMP development could provide a means of encouraging employers and job seekers to make use of employment services. For example, only registered employers who declare their vacancies in the PES could receive support under ALMP programs. These could include (a) providing an exemption from taxes for a fixed period for employers who engage TVET graduates, persons with disabilities, persons from other disadvantaged groups, or the long-term unemployed; and (b) providing graduates with training activities in TVET institutes, private training institutes, or field training through PPPs to adapt the existing labor force to employers' needs, and/or to update and upgrade their skills. This might reduce the informal private sector and, in the longer term, be a source of additional tax income for the country. Encouraging new entrepreneurs at start-up of their business could be done by providing free management courses and an assessment of the viability of micro and small enterprises.

(iv) A better functioning PES is required. Only big companies are bound to declare their vacancies, meaning that the majority of what happens in the labor market remains invisible, while only a minor proportion with declared vacancies and registered job seekers is visible for possible matching.

(v) Regular updating of lists of vacancies and job seekers is needed; otherwise, it is very difficult to assess the efficiency and the results of the PES. A clarification of its mission, additional training for its staff, a strong modification of its services to users and its role among stakeholders are urgently needed, as well as participation in new structures such as sector skills working groups, TVET advisory boards, and others.

(vi) At the regional level, conduct small-scale labor market surveys in prioritized economic sectors while closely working with SSCs in the same selected economic sectors. Regional skills observatories in close cooperation with the PES and the TVET system should be able to better approach the regional or local labor market and assess its current and future needs concerning jobs and skills in demand. In sharing the collected information with career guidance in the TVET sector and career planning services in the PES, this would also reduce the gap and mismatch between labor demand and labor supply.

166. A fully functioning TVET system is critical to ensuring that all students learn from a modern, competency-based curriculum delivered through a better qualified teaching staff to strengthen the current weak links between the educational system and private sector employers. This also means building job-relevant skills that employers demand by implementing selective ALMP, with a focus on discouraged workers and people with disabilities, and to increase the female labor force participation. Furthermore, entrepreneurship and innovation should be encouraged by increasing access to quality tertiary education for motivated TVET graduates, as this route can ensure that higher education graduates also possess skills valued in the market.

V. Strengthening the Relevance and Quality of Technical and Vocational Education and Training in Uzbekistan

167. Section III identified challenges for the Uzbekistan TVET system and section IV considered the system in relation to the labor market. This section suggests options for how to improve the relevance and, thereby, the quality of TVET in Uzbekistan. Stakeholder opinions were gathered about the potential benefits and barriers for implementation of PPP modalities. New and varied approaches to PPPs are essential for the further development of the Uzbekistan TVET system. However, these should be considered in terms of existing and potential partnerships and in the light of international experience. Thus, PPPs are discussed below in section K.

A. Demand for Technical and Vocational Education and Training and TVET Enrollments

168. In accordance with the new program structure, TVET students will come from grade 11 on a voluntary basis. For the TVET system and the local TVET college to get updated and have current information of the demand from employers, establishing sector skills councils (SSC) would be very useful.[82]

169. SSCs are platforms of cooperation in which at least two types of stakeholders are involved: public authorities, social partners (the representative organizations of employers and employees); and education, TVET institutes, and research institutes. The European experience has clearly shown that SSCs work in a structured and continuous way. They are permanent bodies as opposed to something set up on a temporary basis as a reaction to a specific need. The SSCs may operate at national or regional level, depending on the country context. Finally, their existence reflects the shared will to reform TVET to better meet labor market needs.

170. Stakeholder discussions have identified potential benefits of SSCs (creating a more demand-based focus for TVET, reducing misbalances in the labor market, understanding and building relationships with employers, and others) as well as challenges to establishing SSCs in Uzbekistan (difficulties in identifying sectors, difficulties in establishing contact with businesses, need for legal framework, and others) and the types of support needed to establish them (identify leaders [change agents] and networks [involve MOELR and employers] and identify focus for mediation between employers and education, and others).

171. There is already a very good showcase for the further establishment of SSCs in Uzbekistan. This experience covers a wide range of benefits from the development of needed occupational competency standards and curriculum development to support TVET implementation such as entrepreneurship training and the enterprise award. The British Council has planned to expand the activities to three more sectors: agriculture, energy, and construction. It is strongly recommended to further compile experiences gathered from the British Council regarding establishment and functioning of the tourism SSC. These experiences should ensure that the SSC concept can be further disseminated successfully to other sectors.

---

[82] Refer to section III A and B for further situation analysis.

172. SSCs can be used as a tool to aggregate demand for TVET graduates by sector. To ensure that TVET colleges are in line with local demand, further structures are required. As discussed above, two mechanisms for this are suggested: an advisory board and education committees. These structures can be used to facilitate direct communication between local employers and TVET colleges.

173. **Improvements to communication between employers and training providers.** It has been emphasized that there is a strong need for more direct communication between employers and training providers. This can be done by direct personal communication via employer participation in implementation of programs, management support mechanisms, and others. But it is also recommended that regular local surveys among employers are conducted. Many simple web-based tools such as SurveyMonkey can be used to make this exercise as simple and efficient as possible.

174. Seventeen percent of employers in the employer survey indicated that they would like to participate in "identification of needed skills," so there seems to be a need and willingness from employers to engage in identification of required skills. Free economic zones (FEZs) are not involved in identification of required skills, but many of the companies establishing themselves in FEZs communicate directly with local TVET colleges. In the longer term, there could be advantages from a stronger involvement of FEZs in identifying skills demand.

B. Careers Education and Guidance

175. The situation for careers education and guidance (CEG) is not promising. The current understanding of CEG in Uzbekistan is mostly related to activities ensuring that graduates get employed. Examples are job fairs, advice on how to conduct job interviews, and others. This is a narrow definition.[83] Career should be seen as an individual's progression through learning and work. Careers education helps individuals to develop the knowledge and skills they need to make successful choices, manage transitions in learning, and move into work. Careers guidance builds on this in that it enables individuals to use the knowledge and skills developed through careers education to make the decisions about learning and work that are right for them. The purpose of CEG is to develop individuals' competencies to make decisions about learning and work that are right for them. This also implies that CEG is a lifelong process beginning at a very early stage and, in principle, not ending before the work life ends. As the work life changes at an ever-increasing speed, the importance of CEG becomes bigger and bigger.

176. To structure the CEG delivery it is recommended to develop an overall module-based CEG curriculum for students in public schools and TVET colleges. The CEG competencies and curriculum approaches vary globally, but the United Kingdom, for example, has a long tradition of CEG. Their Career Development Institute has together with the Association for Careers Education and Guidance developed a framework for careers and work-related education. The framework covers CEG from 7 to 19 years. The framework includes 17 areas of learning for CEG. The areas are grouped into three broad themes: developing yourself through careers; employability and enterprise education; learning about careers and the world of work, and developing your career management and employability skills. The framework can be used to develop a CEG curriculum suited to the Uzbek labor market and education system.

177. A typical discussion on CEG is on how and where to implement the CEG activities. CEG activities may be spread throughout the curriculum and each teacher incorporates CEG into daily activities and/or a certain

---

[83] Refer to section III C i. for further situation analysis.

time frame is set up for CEG and the activities are formally set out in the curriculum. In principle, CEG should start from early grades. The reform of TVET in Uzbekistan provides a good opportunity to include CEG activities in the vocational parts of grades 10 and 11, but it is recommended to start earlier.

C. Curriculum

178. **Competency-based curriculum.** Initial feedback was sought from stakeholders on the potential introduction of competency-based training (CBT) and the ideas behind a modularized curriculum. Responses were generally positive to the approach outlined below.[84]

179. CBT curricula can be developed in different sequences. The idea of CBT is to link the world of employment with the world of education so that demand and supply are matched in the labor market. The demand comes from employers demanding competencies and the supply comes from TVET graduates and the existing workforce. So, in a well-functioning labor market, the applicants who apply for vacant positions have the competencies that the employers want. For this to happen, the curriculum development process can follow the process outlined in Figure 12.

180. **Occupational competency standards.** The starting point for developing CBT curricula is the occupational competency standard (OCS). This document sets out employment outcomes and the competencies required in the occupation. The OCS is developed by employers, and they are by definition "true." They reflect what the employers demand, so it is not a document for discussion by other stakeholders. As outlined above, typically, the SSCs develop the OCS.

181. The curriculum development group translates the OCS into the learning outcomes in the curriculum. Members of the curriculum development groups usually include curriculum experts, teachers, and employers. The degree of employer involvement can vary. Usually, the curriculum development group drafts the curriculum and employers will then review, comment, and validate the curriculum. The employer survey revealed that 16% of employers are willing to participate in adaptation of curriculum and 15% of employers are willing to participate

Figure 12: **Competency-Based Curriculum Approach**

Figure 13: **The Knowledge, Skills, Attitude Model of Competence**

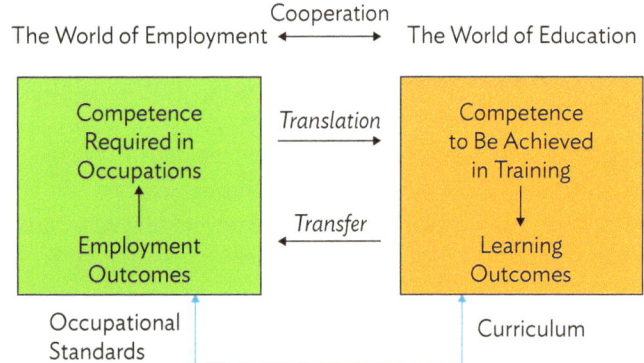

Source: Authors.

Source: Authors.

---

[84] Refer to section III C ii. for further situation analysis.

in development of new curriculum.⁸⁵ These numbers are promising given that the key to effective curriculum development is having employers who are able and willing to participate in the curriculum development process, not just a large number of employers.

182. A core concept of CBT is the notion of competence. Many different definitions are available. An often-used definition is based on knowledge, skills, and attitude as outlined in Figure 13. Only when a student has the knowledge, skills, and attitude is she or he deemed to be competent and to have skills valued in the labor market. One of the problems of the current curriculum and implementation is that it is focused on development of knowledge only.

183. The current curriculum system in Uzbekistan is generally subject-oriented rather than module-oriented. The authors propose that this curriculum be changed to adopt a modular CBT approach. There are many advantages to a modular approach, such as the following:
   (i) It gives employers the flexibility to train their workforce in skills that suit their needs.
   (ii) It allows for curricula to respond quickly to changes in the world of work.
   (iii) It gives learners opportunities to select courses of interest.
   (iv) There are greater opportunities to move in and out of the TVET system.
   (v) It is easier to tailor learning to different learning groups.
   (vi) It can reduce dropouts and increase learners' motivation.⁸⁶

184. Different formats for modules can be used. Different structures for CBT curricula can be found globally. A useful and logical approach is to develop three kinds of competencies: (i) key competencies that should be possessed by all, (ii) competencies that should be possessed by all those in a particular sector, and (iii) competencies that should be possessed by all in the same occupation. This structure is very cost-efficient because, in principle, only one set of key modules, a certain number of sector modules to be used for all programs in the sector, and then specialized modules for each occupation need to be developed. This structure also follows the sector approach, which will make it clearer for the SSC to clarify how they can contribute.

185. Regarding key competencies, different approaches can be used. In Europe, "Key Competences for Lifelong Learning: European Reference Framework" (the framework) was adopted in 2006. It provided a common European reference framework on key competencies to guide policy makers, education and training providers, social partners, and learners. The Council of the European Union launched a review of the framework in 2017, and adopted a new recommendation on key competencies for lifelong learning in May 2018.⁸⁷ The proposal sets out eight key competencies: literacy; languages; mathematics, science, and technology; digital; personal, social, and learning; civic competence; entrepreneurship; and cultural awareness and expression. These key competencies can be used as a starting point for development of key competencies relevant for the Uzbek labor market and context.

186. Stakeholders showed a very positive attitude toward the modular CBT-based curriculum approach, and many benefits were identified for students, teachers, employers, and the TVET system. Discussions also revealed potential challenges to introduction of CBT in Uzbekistan, including the need first to establish centralized structures such as SSCs; develop occupational competency standards and new curricula; and the need to train teachers and masters in CBT and new assessment procedures. Clearly, employer involvement is very much

---

⁸⁵ ADB. Forthcoming. *Skills Needs Assessment for Micro and Small Enterprises in Uzbekistan: Enterprise Survey Report* (footnote 2).
⁸⁶ European Centre for the Development of Vocational Training (Cedefop). 2016. Application of Learning Outcomes Approaches Across Europe: A Comparative Study. *Cedefop Reference Series*. No. 105. Luxembourg: Publications Office. http://dx.doi.org/10.2801/735711.
⁸⁷ The Council of the European Union. 2018. *Council Recommendation on Key Competences for Lifelong Learning*.

needed, and the SSC structure could be the critical condition for successful implementation. The SSC should provide the OCS and should also recognize the curriculum—which they will do if they also have ownership of the process.

187. Decree 5313 gives some direction on the content of the new curriculum. It notes that training should (i) be conducted in skills areas considering the priorities and prospects for economic development, (ii) include practical skills in using modern information and communication technologies and knowledge of at least two foreign languages, (iii) consider the real need for personnel and proposals of employers, and (iv) be conducted with the use of pedagogical processes based on new formats and methods (footnote 24).

D. Teaching Staff

188. This section develops suggestions for improving the competencies of teaching staff in the TVET colleges. Currently, teaching staff are divided into teachers and masters.[88] In CBT, there is no such division between theory and practice. A module will have learning objectives formulated with the prefix: "At the end of this module the learner is able to . . ." The focus is on what the student can do, not what the student knows. Hence, a module mixes theory and practice and the teacher, instructor, or trainer should have both the technical knowledge, as well as the practical experience to deliver the modules. Therefore, it is common in many countries that teachers in TVET colleges are themselves qualified in the occupation or trade they are teaching and they have many years of practical experience (e.g., teachers at construction colleges delivering the carpentry programs would themselves be carpenters).

189. Going forward, it is recommended that the distinction between teacher and master be eliminated to provide for better integration of theory and practice. Such a reform would be controversial because teachers receive higher salaries than masters so this would require remodeling of staff salaries and benefits. Pre-2017, this would have affected the salaries of over 100,000 TVET teaching staff. However, by September 2019, this number had dropped to 34,187, of whom 65% were teachers and 35% were masters (Table 13). Depending on the scale of demand for TVET from AY2020/2021, more teachers and masters will be recruited so it may be possible to effect such changes in the new contracts. However, there are other mechanisms for integrating the learning of theory and practice, so in the short term and medium term, other mechanisms could be piloted, including a recruitment requirement for work experience for new staff or provision of company-based training to existing teachers, as detailed below.

190. One way to introduce more practical and "real world experience" into the TVET colleges is to involve industry people in the training process. Guest lecturing is one of several partnership variations (29% of employers indicate that they are willing to give guest lectures at the local TVET institution). Another variation is to hire industry employees on short-term contracts. A large percentage of employers train their TVET graduates through mentoring by senior staff within the company and by "in-house training (side-by-side-learning)." So, companies do indeed have staff with experience as trainers and mentors. These employees could either be offered contracts or offered further training in pedagogics, planning of training, and others. The competencies gained by the employees will be of benefit not only for the employee's career, but also for the employer. There should be demand for development of such a model and pedagogical training. In the longer term, a closer cooperation between employers and TVET colleges can be developed where more staff and/or longer contracts can be developed. This can be of interest also for employers whose business is seasonal, where the low season can be used by employees to work at colleges.

---

[88] Refer to section III C iii. for further situation analysis.

191. TVET college staff could be sent for internships or employed on short-term contracts in the companies. Most teachers seem to have higher education and not much practical experience. Therefore, short-term internships are critical. Employers who participated in the survey indicated that they were both able and willing to have TVET college staff visiting or being interns in their companies (footnote 2). In the long term, a situation where teachers work some weeks every year in a company will have huge benefits for the teacher and the TVET system. The idea of summer practice can also be applicable for teaching staff; the survey results support the idea of a closer cooperation between companies and TVET colleges on activities that can support the development of the teaching staff.

192. In relation to competencies of TVET college teaching staff, an example of a national occupational competency standard (NOS) for a TVET teacher is as follows. The standard is formulated in four modules with learning objectives and performance criteria for all learning objectives. The overall structure and learning objectives are outlined below. The NOS for a TVET teacher is structured around four modules or units, each with several learning objectives and performance criteria:
   (i)   Work effectively within TVET sector (6 learning objectives and 16 performance criteria);
   (ii) Maintain and enhance professional practice and technical competency (4 learning objectives and 14 performance criteria);
   (iii) Deliver competency-based training (5 objectives and 21 performance criteria); and
   (iv) Support and coach learners (2 learning objectives and 11 performance criteria).

193. The above standard can be used to develop a curriculum for the pedagogical training of TVET college teaching staff, as well as training of in-company trainers, and its implementation can be approached on different levels. In the recruiting phase, the TVET system can develop new criteria for TVET teaching staff based on the NOS. It is recommended to include, for example, 3 years of practical experience in the relevant occupation, as a minimum. Whether or not such candidates are interested in the positions is another question and will most likely be related to the difference between the salaries and benefits in the private and public sectors.

194. For pedagogical training, it is recommended that a modularized curriculum be developed and implemented gradually. Teaching is a conservative profession and many teachers are reluctant to adopt new ways of teaching. What will be required is a gradual introduction of the new systems with training, experimentation with new methods, new training with sharing of experiences, and planning of new experiments. A modular curriculum mixes theory and practice so the trainer needs to have both the technical knowledge and the practical experience to deliver the modules. It is common in many countries that TVET teachers are themselves qualified in the occupation or trade they are teaching. Occupation-specific technical training, especially for those teachers without an industry background, will be essential. A possible structure with a mix of theory and practice could be
   (i)   pre-service training with introduction to CBT, teacher roles, and overview of both theory and practice teaching methods;
   (ii) in-service training with colleagues from other TVET colleges provides opportunities to learn new aspects and share experience, and should be supported with exposure to latest technologies; and
   (iii) development of a support network so that teachers can continue to share experiences and ideas after returning to their own colleges.

195. To supplement the above process, a mentor could be assigned to each new teacher. The mentor could be a more experienced teacher who will participate in the professional development of the new teacher. For all teaching staff, a plan for CPD should be prepared, discussed, agreed with, and followed up by the responsible manager. The mechanism for this can, for example, be an annual "staff development meeting" between the staff and the manager. The purpose of the meeting is development and not control. The CPD plan should be the overarching document guiding this process.

196. To further support the development of TVET college staff competence, a web-based network to connect TVET teaching staff and industry trainers could be set up. Such a network could support the exchange of teaching material, experiences, technological developments, and others.

E. Facilities and Equipment

197. The situation regarding facilities and equipment in the Uzbekistan TVET sector is challenging.[89] The first step in improving the situation could be to clarify what facilities and especially what equipment is needed for the TVET system to be effective. For this task, the SSCs can be of great help. When developing new modularized and CBT-based curriculum, the SSC can be used to identify what the minimum requirements are for equipment. The CBT curriculum sets out the learning objectives and performance criteria that students should meet. This includes practical work on specific equipment. It is an attribute of CBT that it sets the minimum requirements for being competent. However, in many sectors it is not possible for the college to have up-to-date equipment for all aspects of the occupation. There may be several reasons for this. The obvious one is that the equipment is too expensive and therefore simply not available within the TVET college budget. Another reason may be that the technological development for certain equipment is so rapid that a TVET system cannot keep up.

198. Whatever the reason, pragmatism and a sense of realism are needed when preparing plans for updating TVET facilities and equipment; it is imperative to involve employers in addressing these challenges. A way forward is to define the equipment that is "reasonable" to expect that a TVET college can offer students for practical work. In a curriculum with key sector and occupational modules, one can expect that the equipment needed to become competent in the sector modules should be available at the college. But the more specialized the equipment gets, the less likely it is that a college will have it. The situation varies a lot across different sectors and occupations, so it is not possible to set out clear criteria. However, it is possible to involve the SSC and the local companies in the decision on what is needed at each college. This discussion will also make the employers more aware of their responsibility in terms of offering their equipment for training.

199. Different variants of work-based learning (WBL) can be applied to use employers' equipment for training. New CBT curricula should include a much larger practical component; as practice is implemented more and more at the workplace, the smaller the equipment problem becomes. Different models can be implemented from short company visits, where equipment can be demonstrated to students, to longer apprenticeship periods where students work in the companies and, thereby, become proficient in the use of modern and relevant equipment.

200. In many countries, TVET institutes receive new and updated equipment from suppliers under sponsorship agreements. The benefit to suppliers is that if students are trained on certain equipment, they will also recommend this equipment to future employers, and others. One disadvantage of this approach is that students may only be trained in the use of equipment from certain suppliers, but the problem might not be so serious. In the KOICA centers, for example, students are working with Hyundai motors and problem identification equipment. The training received on this equipment, especially when combined with the development of learning skills, will give students competencies that can quickly be adapted to other makes of cars.

201. Another variation of solving the equipment challenge is to develop a few well-outfitted TVET colleges as centers of excellence. These would be provided with specialized equipment and then send students from other colleges to centers of excellence. In this way, the cost of new and updated equipment can be shared among several institutes. Clearly, there is no simple, single solution to solve the equipment challenge, but PPP may be a useful way to both share responsibility and funding and to open up new and creative ways of implementing TVET.

---

[89] Refer to section III C iv. for further situation analysis.

F. Implementation

202. The main challenge to implementation of TVET in Uzbekistan is that teaching involves too much theory and too little practical work.[90] Several actions can be taken to improve this situation. First, the curriculum should be CBT-based and, thereby, focus on what the students can do and not only on what they should know. Second, teachers need to be able to use different teaching methods to develop different kinds of competencies (e.g., instructive, informative, inquiry-based, dialogue, working practicals, work-based learning). Third, the focus should also be on the types and categories of skills to be developed.

203. The next step can be to investigate how teaching is organized in the TVET college. It is well-known that team organization of teachers is very useful for the more practical teaching methods such as project and case methods. As outlined above, the teaching staff in Uzbekistan is divided into teachers and masters. A way forward could be to organize the teaching staff in teams around modules so that several teachers or masters are responsible for modules including both theory and practice. Such an organization is also a useful tool for teachers' CPD, bringing benefits to both the teacher and the learner.

204. **Entrepreneurship training.** For entrepreneurship training, the concept of "virtual companies" is one way to train students in entrepreneurship and management of companies. The concept can be used in a project structure and can include activities like "Business Fair" where groups of students present their products and services in an open fair with parents, families, friends, and others participating. Such activities are suitable for involvement of employers as guest lecturers and/or judges for competitions between virtual companies. The competitive aspect can further be developed into competitions between students from different TVET colleges and even between countries. Nongovernment organizations like Junior Achievement (see for example, www.jaworldwide.org) organize such events.

205. **Internships.** As mentioned earlier, the TVET curriculum includes internships in companies. In future, the internships should be treated like modules in a modularized curriculum. In this way, learning objectives and performance criteria are clear to students, teachers, and not least employers and company trainers. Based on this description the companies can plan, implement, and assess the students during their internship. To further improve the internships, it is recommended to offer pedagogical training to in-company trainers as suggested in the section on teaching staff. This will further increase the quality of the internships.

206. **Apprenticeships** are another form of work-based learning. Internationally, apprenticeships are getting more and more attention and an increasing number of countries are piloting different models of apprenticeship. Some features of quality apprenticeships are relevant and rigorous training both on and off the job; appropriate regulations; social partner's involvement in design and maintenance of training program; compulsory formal assessment and certification; presence of qualified staff or "master trainers"; and presence of supporting institutions (e.g., sector bodies and industrial associations). Apprenticeships can be defined as follows:
    (i) systematic long-term training for a recognized occupation that takes place substantially within an undertaking or under an independent craftsman and should be governed by a written contract and be subject to established standards;[91] and
    (ii) a combination of on-the-job training and school-based education.[92]

---

[90] Refer to section III C iv. for further situation analysis.
[91] International Labour Organization. Paragraph 46 of the Vocational Training Recommendation, 1962 (No. 117).
[92] G20 Task Force on Employment. 2012. *Key Elements of Quality Apprenticeships.* September 27.

207. There are several issues related to apprenticeship in the Uzbekistan context. Challenges include limited tradition of industry engagement in skills development, poor image of apprenticeship, concerns over the use of apprentices as a source of cheap labor, and limited structure of training (and/or weak monitoring) not leading to a qualification. Although there is clear agreement on the overall benefits and opportunities in the apprenticeship model, it is recognized that for the time being, it is too challenging to implement a full-scale apprenticeship-based TVET system in Uzbekistan.

208. Different elements of the apprenticeship system could be examined, including development of legal documents to structure the mechanism. A lot of international experience in what is needed for successful implementation is available. In terms of the time allocation, the KOICA centers are already implementing a kind of dual model involving 4 months of training in a company as part of a 10-month total program training time.

209. Again, the PPP aspects are the most critical components of implementing new modalities for implementation of TVET. The more the employers are involved in the development, planning, implementation, and evaluation of the different models, the higher is the probability of success. It is important to note that there is no one-size-fits-all model, so some might work in one sector, but not in another. Also, the size of companies is of importance. Most companies in Uzbekistan are MSEs and they have a daily reality that differs from large companies. Typically, MSEs are developing much faster than bigger companies so they are usually not able to make long-term plans and/or obligations, but need more flexible modalities.

210. The employer survey gave promising indications of strong employer support for activities, such as guest lecturing, engaging interns, and organizing summer internship opportunities (footnote 2). There is clear potential for further development of PPP in TVET implementation.

G. Assessment

211. Assessment in the current Uzbek TVET system is focused on the assessment of knowledge, including widespread use of written tests.[93]

212. The United Nations Educational, Scientific and Cultural Organization (UNESCO) recommends establishing effective and appropriate assessment systems for generating and using information on learners' achievements. Evaluation of teaching and learning processes, including formative assessment, should be undertaken with the participation of all stakeholders, notably teachers and trainers, representatives of the occupational fields concerned, supervisors, and learners. Learners' overall performance should be assessed using diversified methods of assessment, including self-assessment and peer assessment, as appropriate.

213. Fourteen percent of respondents to the employer survey indicated a willingness to participate in student assessment. In the current system, employers are also involved in the final assessment of the students (footnote 2).

214. Assessment in a CBT system can serve many purposes, including diagnosis of learners' strengths and weaknesses, directing learners' learning process, providing recognition of learning achievement, helping learners make career choices, and assisting employers to determine the competence of employees. It is not only linked to the certification of competencies for modules or for a full program. The current emphasis in Uzbekistan is on summative assessment. Hence, there seems to be opportunities for further development of formative assessment, and this aspect should be embedded in the TVET training.

---

[93] Refer to section III C v. for further situation analysis.

215. Briefly, the assessment process in CBT should include generation and collection of evidence of learners' competence; judging the evidence against defined standards; and recording the assessment results. In a modularized curriculum, each module will include learning objectives, performance criteria, and, quite often, also the assessment method that should be used. It is strongly recommended to include the assessment method in the curriculum. Based on the method, it is then up to the assessor to develop relevant assessment instruments for each learning objective. Overall, CBT uses three assessment forms: (i) written or oral test for assessment of knowledge, (ii) product assessment for assessment of skills, and (iii) performance assessment for assessment of skills and attitude.

216. Training in assessment should be offered to teachers as well as employees involved in the internship in companies. It should emphasize the need to expand the scope and influence of practical exams on the final grade and should develop the assessors' skills in planning and implementing practical tests, as well as in developing different assessment instruments. Once again, the TVET system can benefit from a close relationship to employers and employees in development of the assessment instruments. An example can be to use employees to develop criteria and the assessment sheet for product assessment. It is strongly recommended to develop and pilot the use of logbooks for students' competence development. The logbook approach has a lot of advantages such as simplicity, involvement of employers, and, not least, the involvement of the student in terms of self-assessment and peer assessment and taking responsibility for their own competence development.

H. Graduates

217. The employer survey showed that employers are interested in getting information on graduates (footnote 2). The communication process between companies and the TVET colleges regarding information on students can come through different channels. Anecdotal evidence suggests many companies use internships to assess students before hiring them post-graduation.[94] Thus, in some cases, employers have a good idea of who they would like to hire. In other cases, they do not. Therefore, the process of getting the information about students to the employers should be integrated into CEG activities. Here, the TVET college can play an active part in supporting students and companies, for example, by

    (i)   offering graduates the opportunity to upload resumes and further information to the college's website;
    (ii) offering companies the opportunity to post vacancies on the college's website; and
    (iii) organizing "matchmaking" activities and job fairs where companies can meet potential graduates.

218. Thus, there are many ways in which TVET colleges can support employers and graduates. The closer the cooperation between employers and colleges, the better this process will work. CEG training should also include training on how graduates contact companies, write resumes, and conduct interviews, and others.

219. In the short term, a TVET college is interested in graduates getting employed quickly and, thereby, generating a positive image for the college. But in the longer term, it is crucial for the college to stay in contact with the graduates. Graduates should contribute to development of a positive image of the college. A simple way is to publish newsletters electronically to graduates' e-mail. If the content is interesting and create value for graduates, they will also "spread the message" to colleagues and employers. The employer survey revealed that employers are very interested in receiving news from the TVET system and graduates are a very useful communication tool (footnote 2).

220. Furthermore, the TVET college can create value for graduates by offering simple ways of staying in contact with classmates and other graduates: 17% of male TVET graduates and 12% of female graduates were

---

[94] Refer to section III C vi. for further situation analysis.

recruited via social network (friends, relatives, teachers, and others). Graduates will later need CVET courses to stay updated, so the closer the contact is between the college and the graduates, the easier it is to develop and sell CVET courses to the graduates. The "customer value" of one iVET student can be very high if managed correctly.

221. On a TVET system level, information about graduates via tracer studies and others are likewise crucial for the long-term development of the TVET system. The www.college.mehnat.uz database is already functioning. A systematic approach is needed to ensure that the required information is collected. This will include a more thorough discussion of what the information is needed for and what decisions should be made based on that information.

222. Graduate information should also be made more effective by strengthening the links between local TVET college management and local PES management to establish a better knowledge base of available labor supply and existing (and foreseen) labor demand. A flexible structure is needed for this information exchange, and the collection of data on vacancies needs to be improved in PES. It is always easier to match vacancies with job seekers and new graduates at the local level and users (job seekers, graduates, employers, and other stakeholders) could really benefit from a better mutual knowledge base and shared information between the two institutions.

I. Quality Assurance

223. Uzbekistan operates a system akin to quality control for its TVET system. Inspection and monitoring are carried out to ensure that rules and regulations are followed, the assumption being that if the established system is being applied fully, the expected results will be forthcoming.[95] Internationally, countries are focusing more on quality assurance (QA) systems as a way, not only to monitor quality levels, but also to create systems and pathways for quality improvement at all levels of the system. Quality can be defined in several ways, for example, "Quality is the degree to which an object (entity) (e.g., process, product, or service) satisfies a specified set of attributes or requirements."[96] Using this definition, quality in TVET is achieved when the TVET system satisfies a specified set of requirements (like the current process in Uzbekistan). A QA system should be established.

224. A second definition offers more scope for interpretation in the sense that quality is relative, like high or excellent quality or low or poor quality. And since quality is linked to requirements, a VET system can have a high quality on certain criteria and a lower quality on other criteria. "The quality of something can be defined by comparing a set of inherent characteristics with a set of requirements. If those inherent characteristics meet all requirements, high or excellent quality is achieved. If those characteristics do not meet all requirements, a low or poor level of quality is achieved" (footnote 99). Based on this second definition, QA is a system set in place to avoid poor quality. The system includes quality control and should ideally also contribute to quality improvement.

225. This leads to the question: Why should a country have a QA system for TVET? There are several reasons:
   (i) **Control.** Ensure that training offered meets a minimum quality level so that learners can use the training in a lifelong learning perspective. A condition for this is that qualifications awarded are recognized in the labor market.
   (ii) **Effect.** Ensure that the training delivered is in accordance with the needs of the labor market.
   (iii) **Efficiency.** Ensure that the funds are spent in the most efficient way.
   (iv) **Development.** Ensure that quality is constantly improved.

---
[95] Refer to section III C vii. for further situation analysis.
[96] European Quality Assurance in Vocational Education and Training (EQAVET).

226. In the long run, it must be the overall objective of a QA system to constantly improve the quality of the VET system so that graduates are employed, and employers have access to a qualified workforce that meets their needs. QA in TVET and QA systems come in many different forms. In the European Union, the overarching framework for QA is the European Quality Assurance in Vocational Education and Training (EQAVET). It is recommended to use EQAVET as the initial framework for development of a QA system in Uzbekistan.

227. The main document guiding the European work on QA systems is the European Quality Assurance Reference Framework for Vocational Education and Training.[97] The recommendation introduces a quality and improvement cycle based on a selection of quality criteria, descriptors, and indicators applicable to quality management at both TVET-system and TVET-provider level. The cycle suggested has the phases shown in Figure 14, indicating that QA is an ongoing process.

Figure 14: **Quality Improvement Cycle for Technical and Vocational Education and Training**

Source: Authors.

228. The recommendation sets out the establishment of a Quality Assurance National Reference Point that is "linked to the particular structures and requirements of each Member State and that, in accordance with national practice, brings together existing relevant bodies and involved social partners and all stakeholders concerned at national and regional levels, to ensure the followup of initiatives." As mentioned in section C, MHSSE will establish the QA system in Uzbekistan (together with the State Inspection of Educational Quality), so MHSSE can be considered the national reference point.

229. The work on implementing EQAVET is ongoing. Apart from its own website (https://www.eqavet.eu/), the network has developed two more websites related to the development and implementation of QA at the system level and at the TVET provider level (footnote 99). Each website offers advice and ideas on how to implement QA based on four phases: planning, implementation, evaluation, and review. The websites also offer a glossary, case studies, and a selection of building blocks that can be used in development of the QA system. The building blocks can also be used to further develop the business plan recommended above as well as the work of the TVET Colleges Advisory Board and Education Committees.

230. It is recommended that MHSSE sets out clear and usable criteria for accreditation of TVET colleges. Again, the EQAVET framework can offer inspiration, but criteria should reflect the Uzbekistan labor market and legal framework. The aspect of accreditation becomes even more important when private TVET institutes enter the market.

231. Introducing QA frameworks in WBL, such as internships and apprenticeships, is an important part of any QA system. The EQAVET network has identified a series of common themes, called building blocks, which have been used to establish and strengthen QA processes in WBL in line with EQAVET. These six building blocks support and complement each other and build on the EQAVET indicative descriptors and indicators.

---

[97] EUR-1Lex. Recommendation of the European Parliament and the Council of 18 June 2009 on the Establishment of a European Quality Assurance Reference Framework for Vocational Education and Training.

The building blocks are designed to be useful and appropriate for the three main models of WBL.[98] The building blocks above can be used by the suggested education committees to ensure the quality of the internships.

J. Continuing Vocational Education and Training

232. There is a promising demand for continuing vocational education and training (CVET) in Uzbekistan because of a high need for retraining of TVET graduates and/or demand for continuous professional development of the workforce.[99] The employer survey revealed that some companies find that the current training available is not relevant (footnote 2).

233. Most companies in Uzbekistan are MSEs. In an MSE, employees need to be flexible and multiskilled because there is less specialization than in a bigger company. This means that CVET offers should include both broad and narrow courses. Also, a smaller company would usually prefer shorter duration courses because of less predictability of operations and a lower training budget. The employer survey also showed that some employers find the current CVET offerings too expensive. The above considerations indicate that CVET courses should be very flexible, both in terms of content, timing, and pricing structure.

234. Thus, the market for CVET is very different from iVET. iVET is a business-to-consumer (B2C) market where the customer is the student. The CVET market is both a B2C, but also a business-to-business (B2B) market where the CVET provider markets itself to both individuals and companies.

235. On the supply side, the situation is also different because a TVET college might have a monopolistic position as sole supplier of iVET in a region while there can easily be more suppliers of CVET courses. The market situation is different across sectors. There are very low entry barriers for setting up CVET courses in bookkeeping where you only need a classroom and some computers compared with a CVET course in Computerized Numerical Control programming and production.

236. Compared with iVET, CVET is often considered to be
  (i) delivered by various types of organizations or individual trainers;
  (ii) governed by different sector organizations with large segments being unregulated;
  (iii) market-driven and more focused on immediate needs of businesses or sectors;
  (iv) characterized by informal or nonformal learning and often in-company training;
  (v) short term and not always leading to a full qualification that would certify a comprehensive set of knowledge, skills, and competence;
  (vi) funded by a mixture of public authorities, individuals, and business;
  (vii) less tightly (or not at all) regulated when it comes to curriculum, certification process, qualifications, and the qualifications of delivering the training;
  (viii) based on contractual relationships between the funding organization and the CVET provider. The provider must "compete" for its clients; and
  (ix) restricted to a specific group of people (either those who receive public benefits, those employed in a given sector, or those who pay) as opposed to iVET which is much less targeted and should provide more universal access.[100]

---

[98] EQAVET. 2012. *Quality Assuring Work-Based Learning*. Dublin: EQAVET Secretariat.
[99] Refer to section III D. for further situation analysis.
[100] ICF GHK. 2013. Study on Quality Assurance in Continuous VET and on Future Development of EQAVET.

237. As a result of these differences, the rationale for introduction of government requirements and QA in the fields of CVET can differ from those in the fields of iVET. In CVET, the rationale for introducing QA requirements is often different:

(i) The public sector only funds some aspects of CVET and, therefore, in many instances it only imposes QA requirements on these parts of CVET. Furthermore, the funding is often from different sources (regional, public employment services [PES], education) and the different funding bodies may have the tendency to impose their own requirements which suit their objectives in terms of training and hence what is understood as quality.

(ii) Introducing transparency to "consumers" of CVET "services" is another reason why the state may want to intervene in CVET. In many countries, the policy approach to CVET is based on a liberal model whereby the state does not regulate the market, but tries to make the market more optimal by improving information available to those who purchase CVET.

(iii) Increasingly, with the development of a qualifications system and frameworks that cover CVET, as well as promotion of mechanisms for transfer and recognition of credit, the public authorities stimulate the use of QA mechanisms to support trust in the system.

238. In addition to the above, the developments in QA in CVET are also stimulated from within the private market for training (not only from the side of public authorities). The fact that there is a market for training services with large numbers of small and medium-sized providers means that these actors are searching to signal the trustworthiness, validity, and reliability of their services to many individuals and businesses. Accreditation schemes, QA certifications, and labels are a way of communicating these messages.

239. A CBT-based and modularized structure is recommended for the TVET curriculum. In such a system, it is very easy to adapt modules from iVET to CVET. In the modules, everything is formulated in learning objectives so, in principle, new modules can be quickly developed using learning objectives from one or several modules. Once the TVET colleges have the state curriculum and start developing the local curriculum, they can already start developing their CVET activities.

240. An education committee could be established for each TVET program. One of the tasks of this committee could be to develop the school curricula. It is evident that since the members of the education committee would be employers and practitioners of the occupation, they will also have first-hand knowledge about the CVET demand for the occupation. Thus, they can also be responsible for at least outlining and suggesting modules to be offered as CVET.

241. Whatever the sector, the CVET market is usually more competitive, and the TVET colleges need to act in a very market-responsive way and with a high degree of focus on marketing. This forces each college to develop its marketing staff, which will also benefit its ability to do well in the iVET market. Public–private partnership (PPP) activities and the involvement of the private sector in both an advisory board and an education committee will benefit the TVET college.

242. In the implementation of CVET, the TVET college also must develop new competencies. CVET is almost, by definition, delivered to adults so teaching and training methods should be adapted accordingly. These challenges will also develop the competencies of the teaching staff so, again, a good argument for further development of CVET. When delivering CVET, teaching staff will also come into personal contact with many employees from the private sector. This will increase the teaching staff's personal network and contribute to the TVET college constantly updating its knowledge base. A "positive circle" can be established where the college is able to stay in line with the labor market to be competitive.

243. The CVET activities do not need to be developed and implemented only by one TVET college. TVET colleges from the same sector, but from different regions can easily work together with, for example, an SSC to develop and implement CVET courses. This will further contribute to the development of TVET colleges both on the content side, but also by offering further funding opportunities.

K. Governance and Management

i. Institutional Management

244. The identification of all stakeholders in a college and how to manage the relationships with and between them is one of the tasks of the TVET college management. Stakeholders in each TVET college are students, employers (state-owned industries, private companies), parents, government (economy, budget), society (labor market, export), funding agencies, teachers, and the *khokimyat*. Management and boards of trustees of TVET colleges should also see themselves as institutional stakeholders.[101]

245. TVET college boards of trustees are more akin to advisory boards providing strategic advice to the management as they do not have much of an oversight role. However, the potential benefits of an advisory board are actually manifold: marketing of the institution and its services; piloting of new structures; involving worker organizations; improved training of trainers; involvement in curriculum development; monitoring of the institution (potential QA role).

246. There is a clear need for a more market-oriented approach for the TVET colleges, and it is suggested to involve employee organizations as stakeholders in this approach. In considering different organizational structures of TVET colleges, specific attention must also be given to the potential role of a marketing department and why a marketing department is needed to attract students.

247. **Advisory boards.** More communication between the different levels of the education system is needed. Using European Union TVET systems as a baseline, including how much of the TVET system is funded by employers, a long-term goal for employer funding could be formulated at 25%. From the employer survey, 15% of employers want to participate actively in the management of the local college (i.e., as member of an advisory board) (footnote 2). This is very promising and a strong signal that should be followed up on.

248. In the short term, the current board of trustees should not be replaced by an advisory board, but the concept of an advisory board could be piloted and then later it can be decided whether to merge the two structures or keep two separate structures. The establishment of an advisory board will ensure that relevant stakeholders and employers will have direct access to and influence on the TVET college activities.

249. **Education committees.** To further support the labor market relevance, an education committee could be established for each program offered by the TVET college. The members of the education committee should be representatives from employers and employees. In addition, the person responsible for the program, teacher representatives, and student representatives could also be involved. Selection criteria should be established for all positions, whether for the advisory board or education committee, and proportions of public–private membership established, as well as ensuring a good gender balance.

250. The role of the education committee is to ensure local connection to the labor market at the operational level and is not strategic like the advisory board. The main role of the education committee is to develop the

---

[101] Refer to section III C viii. for further situation analysis.

local school curriculum together with the pedagogical council. Thereby, the local curriculum will be reviewed at least once a year and will immediately be adapted to the local circumstances. As a part of the curriculum, the committee should also clarify the needed minimum technical and staff requirements to implement the curriculum. This information will then go to the management and advisory board and become a part of the business plan. The committee should also be responsible for the quality of the internships by setting up criteria for companies implementing the internships. In addition, the committee could be involved in the use of industry people as guest lecturers, as well as for implementation of teachers' CPD plans. The committee should have a minimum number of annual meetings for review and validation of the curriculum, but could also meet ad hoc depending on the needs.

251. **Marketing.** It is recommended to introduce a marketing department in each TVET college to support its market orientation. The college business plan will set out the overall marketing objectives and the budget, but implementation should be done by TVET college staff. Depending on the size of the institution, it can be a department with several employees or it can be one person. Templates for marketing plans, website design, use of social media, and others could be developed centrally and provided to colleges as the basis for training of marketing staff.

ii. Business Sector Inputs and Public–Private Partnership Modalities

252. PPPs are often mentioned as one of the most important parts of any TVET system. UNESCO's "Recommendation Concerning Technical and Vocational Education and Training (TVET)" sets out 60 separate recommendations under seven different headlines.[102] PPP is mentioned already in point 12: "member states expanding TVET at secondary, post-secondary and tertiary levels as appropriate to their education and training systems and authorities should ensure that there is an institutional framework to engage labor market stakeholders, that qualifications and curricula are developed in consultation with relevant stakeholders, and that programs and qualifications are transparent and quality assured."

253. A separate part of the recommendation is devoted to "social dialogue, private sector and other stakeholders' involvement." The key issues are "social dialogue," "social partners," "private sector," and that large, medium-sized, small, micro, and household enterprises should be involved. The term PPP thus comes in different variations.

254. As early as in 2012, the ADB skills forum highlighted the importance of moving from policy to practice and translating promising polices that have been implemented in advanced countries into concrete actions in developing countries. The skills forum's brief in its table 2 sets out issues and areas for action, "how to" and examples of ADB projects. Examples of issues and how to approach them are outlined in Table 24.

255. Whichever definition and practices are adopted, PPP offers huge opportunities to improve the Uzbek TVET system. To ensure that the PPP activities are relevant, feasible, and sustainable, they must be implemented step by step. A top–down approach would suggest to first establish TVET system mechanisms like NQF and then set up needed structures toward the labor market. This is not recommended because PPP is a new approach in Uzbekistan and it is hard to anticipate which type of the many possible PPP activities will be of use for Uzbekistan. It is, therefore, recommended to use a bottom–up approach where activities are developed as close to the labor market as possible. Furthermore, it would be sensible to start piloting PPP in selected sectors. As in Table 24, the aim should be to focus skills development in sectors that are identified as leaders for the country's competitiveness and align skills development policies with economic and industrial policies.

---

[102] UNESCO. 2016. Recommendation Concerning Technical and Vocational Education and Training (TVET). Paris.

Table 24: Moving from Policy to Practice

Issues and Areas for Action	Approaches
Developing skills required for economic growth and moving from low- to middle-income and from middle- to high-income levels	• Focus skills development in sectors that identify as leaders for the country's competitiveness and align skills development policies with economic and industrial policies
Strengthening the base of higher-order skills in the workforce	• Invest in science, technology, engineering, and mathematics at secondary and post-secondary education levels. Invest in post-secondary and tertiary skills with appropriate qualifications that attract students
Enhancing private sector participation and partnerships to scale-up training provision and increase relevance of training and job placements	• Provide skill vouchers to finance training of target groups by private sector providers • Establish training contracts with private providers with placement-based payments • Develop skills assessment systems that incorporate industry requirements
Increasing opportunities for training for the disadvantaged and promoting TVET for inclusive growth	• Undertake affirmative action to increase access to training for students and workers from poor and disadvantaged backgrounds • Support training of workers for the informal labor markets • Increase opportunities for training in high-growth sectors for the rural youth
Strengthening soft skills, language skills, and ICT skills along with technical skills to improve job readiness	• Incorporate into the curriculum the teaching of soft skills and ICT skills at the secondary stage with appropriate assessment mechanisms
Developing skills development pathways that enable acquisitions of training and updating of qualifications	• Introduce modular training programs for skills updating and upgrading • Put in place recognition of prior learning and pathways between formal and informal learning and institutional and workplace-based training • Develop qualifications based on competencies required by industry
Improve employment services and job placements	• Reform and privatize employment exchanges; focus on ancillary services that link training with actual job placement

ICT = information and communication technology, TVET = technical and vocational education and training.
Source: ADB. 2012. *Adapted from Skills Development: Promising Approaches in Developed Countries and Emerging Economies*. In ADB International Skills Development Forum held in Manila in December 2012.

256. This approach also fits well with the establishment of free economic zones where state-of-the-art production technology is implemented. This will lead to strong employer demand for highly skilled TVET graduates in sectors that are "leaders of the country's competitiveness."

VI. Development Partner Assistance to Technical and Vocational Education and Training and the Labor Market

257. Several international organizations are supporting skills development in Uzbekistan, generally linked with labor market initiatives. Table 25 summarizes these inputs.

Table 25: Development Partner Assistance to the Technical and Vocational Education and Training Sector

Development Partner	Name of Operation	Duration (fiscal year)	Executing Agency	Amount (million)	Project Description
World Bank	Strengthening Social Security Project	2019–2023	MOELR	$50.0	A project on social protection and labor market policies improvement to strengthen the social security system in the country. Project has a component for creating labor market information system.
UNDP	Promoting Youth Employment in Uzbekistan	2019–2021	MOELR	$1.0	Financed by Russian Federation–UNDP Trust Fund for Development to promote youth employment through active labor market policies and support youth entrepreneurship skills development and business start-ups, particularly among university and college graduates, young women, returning migrants, and other vulnerable groups.
European Union	Skills Development for Employability in Rural Areas of Uzbekistan	2019–2022	DTVET Dept., MOA	€10.0	Project supports skills development in agriculture. In May 2019, the EU decided to collaborate with the UNESCO Tashkent office for this project implementation. Project will support TVET policy implementation reform, modernize governance arrangements, and strengthen agriculture and irrigation sectors to serve the needs of the labor market.
KOICA	KOICA Professional Training Centers	2012–2019	MOELR	$18.9	Three PTCs established in Tashkent, Samarkand, and Shakhrisabz cities (total cost: $18.9 million). Two additional PTCs to be built in Fergana and Urgench cities. PTCs train unemployed job seekers with the skills needed by employers in the areas of machinery engineering, automotive production and repair, electrical engineering, and ICT.
Swiss Development Cooperation	Professional Skills Development Project (Phase I–IV)	2004–2018	Former CSSVE	N/A	SDC in close cooperation with the Center for Vocational Education (now DTVET) aimed to develop and implement a model of cooperation between enterprises and vocational colleges to better meet the needs of the labor market and employers. Project developed curriculum and training materials for preparing specialists in hydro melioration and water supply, housing and communal services, automotive production, and entrepreneurship development.
	Skills Development Project	N/A	N/A	N/A	SDC supports the reform of the vocational education sector in Uzbekistan through the development of synergies between the educational process and labor market demands, including improved cooperation between key ministries and agencies in the cycle "Demand–Training–Job Placement" for water-sector professions, and adoption of training programs for two professions of the water supply sector is adopted and required specialists trained in both the secondary specialized education system and the adult further education system.

(continued on next page)

(Table 25 continued)

Development Partner	Name of Operation	Duration (fiscal year)	Executing Agency	Amount (million)	Project Description
GIZ	Professional Education and Vocational Training in Central Asia – Fostering Systemic Approaches in the Food Processing Sector (PECA)	2019–2022	MHSSE	N/A	In this regional project, GIZ supports the modernization of vocational education and training in the food processing sector in Uzbekistan, Kazakhstan, the Kyrgyz Republic, and Tajikistan by strengthening the capacity of Central Asian vocational education systems to train qualified managers and specialists, taking into account the existing needs for economic growth sectors in the region.
British Council	Skills for Employability	2018–2020	DTVET, MOA, MOC, energy and mining, tourism	$0.25	British Council and DTVET, in partnership with Chamber of Commerce and Industry, and youth movement support national reforms in TVET by strengthening links between education and industry, and equipping youth with the skills and competencies that employers require. Support provided to MHSSE and line ministries or responsible agencies of tourism, agriculture, energy and mining, and construction. Aims to reinforce the legislative implementation and set up sound coordination mechanisms on policy design, monitoring, and reporting; train MHSSE staff in the management of TVET providers; introduce new service models such as coaching for improving employment outcomes; and review and redesign active labor market measures in these four sectors.
UNESCO	Skills for Tourism	2014–2018	Former CSSVE, tourism	$0.25	Project supported national reforms in TVET in tourism sector. Key outcomes: (i) development of a work competency framework; (ii) embedding the framework into the system as a basis for development of National Occupational Standards; (iii) creating Sector Skills Councils in tourism and hospitality in Uzbekistan; (iv) senior level policy discussions, study visits, training, professional development.
	Teacher ICT Competency Improvement Project	2015–2018	Former CSSVE	Around $0.50	Priority areas of intervention were education sector policy advice, teacher training, competency-based curriculum development, quality assurance, gender equality, improvement of learning outcomes particularly through using ICT and lifelong learning. Also included capacity building of DTVET.
	Uzbekistan TVET Policy Review Initiative	2018	Former CSSVE	N/A	Skills sector assessment report emphasized the need for development of national qualification framework (NQF), which will further guide the detailed development of the NQF.

CSSVE = Center for Secondary Specialized Vocational Education, DTVET = Department of Technical and Vocational Education and Training of MHSSE, EU = European Union, GIZ = Deutsche Gesellschaft für Internationale Zusammenarbeit, ICT = information and communication technology, KOICA = Korea International Cooperation Agency, MHSSE = Ministry of Higher and Secondary Specialized Education, MOA = Ministry of Agriculture, MOC = Ministry of Construction, MOELR = Ministry of Employment and Labour Relations, N/A = not available, NQF = national qualification framework, PTC = professional training center, TVET = technical and vocational education and training, UNDP = United Nations Development Programme, UNESCO = United Nations Educational, Scientific and Cultural Organization.

Source: Information provided to the authors from the respective agencies.

VII. Conclusion

258. Skills development in Uzbekistan faces many challenges. While sweeping changes are being made, the existing TVET system does not sufficiently equip young people with the essential competencies and skills required for lifelong learning and employment. This results in many young people trying to enter the labor market with weak skill sets and/or competencies that are not relevant to the changing needs of employers. Employers and their businesses are constrained by insufficient numbers of semiskilled and skilled workers in the workforce. Opportunities for continued training or retraining to different occupations are insufficient to requirements, with very few opportunities currently available to participate in retraining at modern professional training centers. The COVID-19 pandemic has had a huge impact on skills development. Apart from the health and economic issues, teachers and learners have been challenged to adopt remote learning and other strategies to reduce human contact. Uzbekistan faces the need for a digital leap which will impact all walks of life. New technologies and new approaches to business, social, and health services need new skills and the TVET sector must adapt quickly to identify them and plan their delivery to learners. In particular, mastery of digital competencies and technical skills, learning skills, and innovation skills are essential in today's world.

259. There is clearly broad provision of TVET programs, some of which are relevant to the needs of large, especially state-owned, enterprises, but few of the programs are aligned with modern employer needs, in particular, regarding the needs of MSEs. There is little contribution to skills definition and monitoring from the private sector, leading to a lack of occupational standards in most professions. Thus, competencies are not well-defined (if at all) which, in turn, translates to weak targeting and effectiveness of the training programs that do exist. As a result of technological advances, there is a high demand for the retraining of workers with out-of-date qualifications, but few locations for the provision of relevant training or assessment.

260. Systemic challenges include the need for better collaboration between employers on the demand side and authorities and institutions on the skills supply side. Linking strengthened labor market institutions and systems with improved PPP-based support to curriculum and program development to the professional training process will create opportunities to equip young people and the unemployed with the essential competencies. Establishment of sector skills councils linked to skills observatories at regional and national levels and combined with reforms of the public employment service and the provision of training to labor services officials is needed. Progress is already being made in strengthening the labor market information systems and the way in which they are used, but further assistance is needed in the form of strengthened labor management and public employment services for them to capture data from MSEs, as well as from the informal sector, and to be able to provide relevant and timely information to job seekers at the local levels. This should be linked to development and delivery of a curriculum for careers education and guidance.

261. Currently gathered data for monitoring, evaluation, and planning labor market needs are inadequate and its reliability is questionable. Strengthened central capacity to train, plan, gather, and handle the data is urgently needed through support to key organizations at national and regional levels, such as the National Scientific Center for Employment and Labor Protection under MOELR and the Institute for Innovative Development, Advanced Training and Retraining of Teaching Personnel of the Vocational Education System. This should

include assistance in the preparation of modularized management training materials and delivery of the training, collaboration with recognized international workforce development agencies, and study tours.

262. Focusing on the institutional level, weaknesses in quality of programs should be addressed through adoption of a competency-based, modularized training approach combined with development of occupational competency standards and upgrading of curriculum and curriculum materials to meet the changing needs of the labor market. These should be linked to new QA and job certification initiatives for both PTC and TVET programs, as well as to capacity building for management and teaching personnel of TVET colleges and PTCs, and PES offices. Upgrading of facilities and equipment needs to go hand in hand with development of curriculum and delivery, perhaps with the establishment of centers of excellence as models for the system.

263. On an individual level, a social marketing campaign should be linked to a new curriculum for careers education and guidance to permit informed decision-making for students and parents on routes into and within the labor market. This could be linked to a second campaign to increase the prestige of TVET training and increase the involvement of the private sector in TVET and professional training. Training provision for vulnerable groups must be strengthened to ensure inclusivity of industrial development, including support for girls to enroll in TVET programs in nontraditional occupational areas. Focused support should be provided for a program to increase the employability of people from vulnerable groups, and to strengthen and expand the current program promoting self-employment through entrepreneurship support to selected TVET graduates.

264. Demand for TVET programs is declining rapidly during the immediate future, with many colleges destined to be closed, but the demand for skilled graduates will remain high. The reduction in current demand must also be seen as a window of opportunity in relation to implementation of the reforms. The new government policies place great emphasis on making TVET programs more competency-based, with focus on a better balance between theory and practical work, greater focus on skills development (nontechnical skills as well as technical), entrepreneurship as a cross-cutting domain, and better-monitored work practice and internships, thus changing the entire TVET sector into a learner-oriented and competency-based delivery system. In terms of leadership of the necessary changes, both government and development partner policies support the needed reform processes. Skills development has been one of the five pillars in the Uzbekistan National Action Strategy on Five Development Priority Areas 2017–2021, which has driven a series of reforms and changes in education and labor market, and education is one of the five pillars of the ADB 2030 strategy.

Glossary

adult education	Education targeting individuals who are regarded as adults by the society to which they belong to improve their technical or professional qualifications, further develop their abilities, enrich their knowledge with the purpose to complete a level of formal education, or to acquire knowledge, skills, and competencies in a new field or to refresh or update their knowledge in a particular field. This also includes what may be referred to as "continuing education," "recurrent education," or "second chance" education.
apprenticeship	Systematic long-term training for a recognized occupation that takes place substantially within an undertaking or under an independent craftsman and should be governed by a written contract and be subject to established standards. Apprenticeships are a combination of on-the-job training and school-based education.
assessment: college-based	Assessment which is developed within the college and is conducted by teachers on an ongoing basis. Tasks that are often included in college-based assessment are assignments, research, presentations, reports, quizzes, and practical activities. This form of assessment provides an opportunity to measure skills and other aspects of performance that cannot be determined by examinations alone.
assessment: external	Examinations set by institutions external to a school and summative in nature. Examples of external assessment include national examinations, Programme for International Student Assessment (PISA), and other international tests.
assessment: formative	Assessment used to inform learning and teaching. Also known as "assessment for learning."
assessment: student	A process by which students are evaluated on their knowledge, skills, and/or ability.
assessment: summative	Assessment that gauges what students have learned over time. Summative assessment is related to the broader learning goals that can be achieved. Sometimes called "assessment of learning."
competency-based technical and vocational education and training	Competency-based TVET is a way to create opportunities for students and workers to develop integrated, performance-oriented capabilities to address working problems and processes in practice, in a meaningful learning environment.
continuing education	See "adult education."

Glossary

continuing vocational education and training (CVET)	Technical and vocational education and training specifically targeting individuals who have undergone some form of initial education to improve their technical or professional qualifications, further develop their abilities, enrich their knowledge with the purpose to complete a level of formal education, or to acquire knowledge, skills, and competencies in a new field or to refresh or update their knowledge in a particular field.
curriculum	Teaching plan, describing content and objectives for subjects.
external quality assurance (EQA)	Considers quality issues from outside an institution. It is often used to ensure compliance with national standards or may be used for evaluation purposes.
gross enrollment ratio (GER)	The number of students enrolled at a given level of education, regardless of age, expressed as a percentage of the official school age population corresponding to the same level of education.
initial education	Formal education of individuals before they enter the labor market. It thus targets individuals who are regarded as children, youth, and young adults by the society to which they belong. It is typically provided by educational institutions in a continuous educational pathway.
initial vocational education and training (iVET)	Formal technical and vocational education of individuals before they enter the labor market. It thus targets individuals who are regarded as children, youth, and young adults by the society to which they belong. It is typically provided by educational institutions in a continuous educational pathway.
internal quality assurance (IQA)	Considers quality issues from within an institute. It is often context, input, process, and/or output based, and is managed from within the institute.
National Occupational Standard (NOS) elements	A unit of NOS must comprise (i) title: the content of the NOS; (ii) overview: an introductory section summarizing the NOS to help the user judge whether it is relevant to them; (iii) performance criteria: defining in detail what is expected of the individual; and (iv) knowledge and understanding: what the individual needs to know and/or understand to enable them to meet the performance criteria. NOS may also have sections covering (i) scope: the range of circumstances or situations that have a critical impact on the activity when carrying out the performance criteria; (ii) elements: a unit of NOS can be divided into two or more discrete elements which describe the activities the person has to carry out; and (iii) values and behaviors: personal attributes an individual is expected to demonstrate within the NOS (United Kingdom [UK] Commission for Employment and Skills and the Federation for Industry Sector Skills and Standards).
National Qualifications Framework	Set of agreed principles, procedures, and standardized terminology intended to ensure effective comparability of qualifications and credits within a country.
net enrollment ratio (NER)	The total number of students in the theoretical age group for a given level of education enrolled in that level, expressed as a percentage of the total population in that age group.
Occupational Standards Framework	Specifies national standards of performance that people are expected to achieve in their work, and the knowledge and skills they need to perform effectively.

portfolio	A collection of student work that demonstrates student progress over time. It is a common method of recording continuous assessment. Portfolios provide teachers, parents, administrators, and prospective employers with evidence of student abilities.
postsecondary nontertiary education	Provides learning and educational activities, building on secondary education, preparing for both labor market entry as well as tertiary education. It typically targets students who have completed upper secondary (ISCED level 3), but who want to increase their opportunities either to enter the labor market or to progress to tertiary education. Programs are often not significantly more advanced than those at upper secondary as they typically serve to broaden rather than deepen knowledge, skills, and competencies. It, therefore, aims at learning below the high level of complexity characteristic of tertiary education.
public–private partnership (PPP)	This assessment adopts a broad definition of PPPs for skills development as any type of institutionalized collaboration between the public and private sectors that aims to develop the skills of students, of the workforce, and/or the public.
PPP framework	The public–private partnership framework considers aspects of policy (joint formulation of skills policies and legislation; joint monitoring and evaluation of their implementation); system (identification of skills demand; development of skills or competency-based standards and qualifications); establishment of mechanism for assessment and certification; establishment of mechanisms for workplace learning (including apprenticeship) and training delivery (provision of workplace learning (apprenticeships); joint assessment and certification of skills; and joint management of training institutions.
quality assurance	Quality assurance is a component of quality management; it is focused on providing confidence that quality requirements will be fulfilled.
quality assurance for VET	A quality assured TVET system ensures that the provision of VET meets the skill and education needs of industry and individuals in changing national, regional, and globalized economic situations.
Sector Skills Council (SSC)	Mechanism for developing dynamic and demand-based TVET planning. Helps establish a common understanding of skills required for specific occupations to meet the requirements of the labor market through links between TVET providers and industry.
standards: achievement	Specified percentages of students expected to achieve an acceptable level of performance in each course of studies. Achievement standards will reflect reasonable expectations pertinent to specific groups of schools and students. All measurements of achievement standards will be related directly to the outcomes and goals stated in the curricula and associated frameworks.
standards: assessment	Criteria adopted for measuring student performance relative to curriculum standards.
standards: curriculum	Statements of general and specific knowledge, skills, and value standards of students. Statements of knowledge, skills, understanding, and learning expected at each grade level. These standards are established during the process of curriculum development and are found in the teaching and learning plans produced for each subject at each grade level.

Glossary

standards: education and pedagogy	General and special knowledge, skills, and value standards of children; standards of knowledge, skills, and values for a profession of a teacher and preschool teacher and their further professional development; competence standards for a managing director of an institution or principal, education inspector, and educational advisor; Textbooks and teaching tools and materials for quality standards.
standards: occupational competency	Statements providing a common understanding of the skills required for specific occupations, based on analyses of the functions and tasks pertaining to each occupation. In particular, occupational competency standards help meet the need to match the requirements of the labor market through common understanding of skills required for specific occupations; in particular, the need to match the requirements of the labor market through the links between TVET providers and industry.

www.ingramcontent.com/pod-product-compliance
Lightning Source LLC
Chambersburg PA
CBHW061142230426
43662CB00029B/2474